Radical Therapy for Software Development Teams

Lessons in Remote Team Management and Positive Motivation

Gregory Lind
Maryna Mishchenko

Apress®

Radical Therapy for Software Development Teams: Lessons in Remote Team Management and Positive Motivation

Gregory Lind
Oregon City, OR, USA

Maryna Mishchenko
Kharkiv, Ukraine

ISBN-13 (pbk): 979-8-8688-0186-0
https://doi.org/10.1007/979-8-8688-0187-7

ISBN-13 (electronic): 979-8-8688-0187-7

Managing Director, Apress Media LLC: Welmoed Spahr
Acquisitions Editor: Shivangi Ramachandran
Development Editor: James Markham
Project Manager: Jessica Vakili

Cover designed by eStudioCalamar

Distributed to the book trade worldwide by Springer Science+Business Media New York, 1 New York Plaza, Suite 4600, New York, NY 10004-1562, USA. Phone 1-800-SPRINGER, fax (201) 348-4505, e-mail orders-ny@springer-sbm.com, or visit www.springeronline.com. Apress Media, LLC is a California LLC and the sole member (owner) is Springer Science + Business Media Finance Inc (SSBM Finance Inc). SSBM Finance Inc is a **Delaware** corporation.

For information on translations, please e-mail booktranslations@springernature.com; for reprint, paperback, or audio rights, please e-mail bookpermissions@springernature.com.

Apress titles may be purchased in bulk for academic, corporate, or promotional use. eBook versions and licenses are also available for most titles. For more information, reference our Print and eBook Bulk Sales web page at http://www.apress.com/bulk-sales.

Any source code or other supplementary material referenced by the author in this book is available to readers on GitHub. For more detailed information, please visit https://www.apress.com/gp/services/source-code.

Printed on acid-free paper

This book is dedicated to and inspired by the many amazing colleagues, mentors, and friends I've had the good fortune to work with over the last 20+ years. From collaborations with government agencies and startups to contributions in open source projects and enterprise ventures, I am profoundly thankful for every opportunity and every individual who generously shared their knowledge. Each one has left an indelible mark on the principles and insights within these pages. As we move forward, I eagerly anticipate continued learning and knowledge exchange within our expanding community, where small businesses and startups are driven by a passion for innovation and excellence.

Above all, I extend my heartfelt gratitude to my friends and family. Despite my often demanding schedule, filled with travel and long hours, their unwavering support has remained constant. Their understanding and encouragement have been the foundation upon which this journey has been built.
—Gregory

I am deeply grateful to my family and friends for their unwavering support. The people who worked with me at the beginning of my journey – in a nonprofit organization and a software development company – and helped underrepresented communities gain the best practices of development and teamwork became the inspiration for this book. I'm grateful to my mentor, who believed in me, the person who continues to support me in all my beginnings. It's crucial to feel supported and surrounded by people who can share knowledge, experience, and empathy when needed.
—Maryna

Table of Contents

About the Authors

With over two decades of professional experience, **Gregory Lind's** career has traversed every facet of software development. He has delved into realms ranging from web design, HTML/CSS, and DevOps to back-end engineering, data administration, project management, and team leadership. This journey culminated in assuming roles within the C-Suite of developer-focused startups. While the majority of his tenure has been dedicated to nonprofit and government-oriented startups, his commitment to open source principles has remained unwavering. Throughout his journey, he's consistently championed open source methodologies, tools, and values, integrating them into every phase of his work.

Maryna Mishchenko started her career at Open Build, a nonprofit that helps underrepresented communities learn programming and initiate their software journey. Her journey stands as a testament to merging technical prowess with a passion for community improvement.

CHAPTER 1

Introduction to Radical

Unveiling the Power of Radical Transparency

In the heart of the software and tech industry, a tale of two approaches unfolds – one shrouded in secrecy and the other thriving on openness. The first scenario paints a picture of a proprietary system where decisions were made behind closed doors. A select few dictated the direction, withholding insights from the very users, developers, and managers who would be impacted. This confined strategy seemed enticing in theory, promising control and exclusivity. Yet, as reality set in, the pitfalls emerged. Delays occurred, errors crept in unnoticed, and the end product bore little resemblance to what was needed.

This story of a closed environment resonates with experiences witnessed across industries. From the catastrophic failure of the Theranos scandal to the fiasco of Volkswagen's emissions scandal, hidden intentions often lead to disaster. A study by Transparency International showed that companies with low transparency scores were more prone to unethical behavior and financial misconduct (`www.transparency.org/en/press/ti-study-finds-the-worlds-biggest-companies-need-to-be-a-lot-more-transpare`). In software development, this lack of transparency can result in software that fails to meet user needs, leading to dissatisfaction and lost resources.

© Gregory Lind, Maryna Mishchenko 2024
G. Lind and M. Mishchenko, *Radical Therapy for Software Development Teams*,
https://doi.org/10.1007/979-8-8688-0187-7_1

Contrast this with open source projects that embody the spirit of collaboration and transparency. The Linux kernel, for instance, is an exemplar of a collaborative approach, fostering innovation through open dialogue and shared decision-making. Studies have shown that open source software exhibits fewer defects and higher quality due to the collective effort of developers worldwide. This approach also generates a community around the project, and as long as the community is managed with guidelines that allow for respectful collaboration and contribution, the diversity of ideas can grow the project in ways the originators may have never imagined.

What if we could take these lessons and apply them universally in software development? What if we shifted from a secretive proprietary model to one where transparency was the cornerstone – embracing open source principles, freeing up communication, and building positive internal and external communities? This book is your guide to unmasking the potential of radical transparency in software development, for your product teams and throughout your organization. By integrating feedback loops, open communication, and inclusive decision-making, we can create products that are not just functional, but adaptive and transformative.

Throughout these pages, we'll explore real-world examples from successful open source projects and internal or proprietary projects being built with radical transparency. We'll examine how companies that practice transparency have cultivated positive cultures that breed trust and innovation. We'll dissect the shortcomings of proprietary approaches that ignore transparency and reveal the practical steps to embrace openness and collaboration. This book is an invitation to rewrite the narrative of software development, product management, and organization hierarchies and processes in general – one where every stakeholder's voice is heard, decisions are made collectively, and innovation is unbounded by secrecy. Let's embark on this journey to harness the power of radical transparency, transforming how we build software and shaping the future of our industry and many others.

Hello and welcome to radical therapy, a guide and tool to help you bring some much-needed sunshine into the often cloudy world of software development, cloud-native applications, and agile projects in general. The ideas in here are not just for software, but that's the "use case" we will apply. Any team or set of teams that work from a business side and technical side and have to interact can benefit from this book and the learning within. What we hope you really get out of this is an idea of how to keep you and the rest of your team, whatever role you play in it, motivated, excited, and productive.

Now, you might be thinking: "Therapy? For software developers? Isn't that a bit... out there?" But hear me out. In today's fast-paced and constantly changing world of technology, it's more important than ever to take care of your mental health and well-being. And that's where radical therapy and more importantly radical transparency comes in. By fostering a culture of openness, honesty, and positivity in your team, you can create a work environment where everyone feels empowered to do their best work and grow both personally and professionally. And the best part? You don't have to sacrifice creativity or innovation to do it. In fact, most teams see a dramatic increase in productivity as well as increase in the longevity of their teams through the retaining of talent.

In this book, we'll explore the latest research and techniques from the world of modern psychology and combine them with adaptive and iterative processes and tools to help you build a team that's both happy and productive. We'll talk about setting and meeting expectations, fostering a growth mindset, and creating a self-managed development process that allows for flexibility and creativity while still maintaining structure. So buckle up, friends, and get ready for a radical journey to software development nirvana.

Starting Chapter 1, we will introduce you to a pair of radical therapists; they will be your guide through the tool as one therapist will be the skeptic of the idea of transparency and positivity in the workplace and instead want to stick with the old and tested methods. Meanwhile, the second therapist will be making the argument for radical transparency, positive feedback, ethical AI, and treating your product more like an open source project. Hopefully, they will bring a bit of levity to the more technical details as well as prepare you for any skeptics in your organization as you hopefully make the argument for radical therapy and joining the community.

Some Tools and an Example
Embracing Radical Transparency in an Example Process

Discover how to integrate radical transparency through an illustrative process influenced by successful open source projects. Dive into a methodology that nurtures open communication, stresses the significance of daily updates, prioritizes thorough documentation and robust testing, encourages early user engagement, fosters transparent code discussions and reviews, aligns with organizational goals, and gains inspiration from real-world instances.

As we start to introduce the concepts and ideas around radical transparency, we will use the examples of software development a lot, and specifically, we will highlight the successes this process has brought to open source projects, as well as the failure of projects that weren't transparent enough.

To start, let's go over some needed culture and process tools with cited examples of their successes.

Cultivating Open Communication

Implementing radical transparency starts with nurturing an environment of candid communication. Business and technical teams engage in regular virtual stand-up meetings using tools like Slack, making sure that every team member, irrespective of their geographical location, feels equally valued (Figures 1-1 and 1-2). These stand-ups transcend mere status updates and create an atmosphere where remote and local teams are seamlessly integrated, fostering a unified sense of purpose. The primary goal is to reduce redundant tasks, remove blocks from completing important tasks, and ensure everyone upstream and downstream is aware, but not interfering with the work being done. They should also be done quickly and facilitate additional discussion where needed.

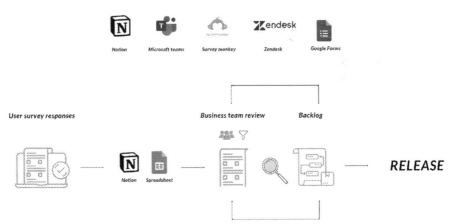

Figure 1-1. *User surveys post-release*

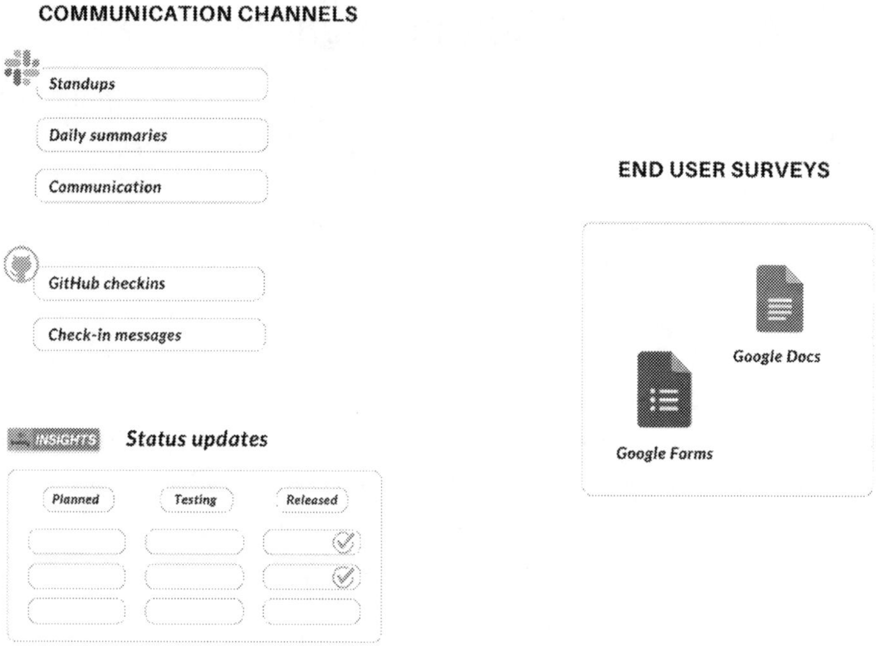

COMMUNICATION CHANNELS

Figure 1-2. *Communication channels*

In the radical transparency version, you should focus on what's next and blocks... not what you did yesterday. This isn't a competition to see who completed what the fastest, it's about being on the same page and helping out where we can.

Benefits of Regular Stand-Up Meetings:

- Cross-functional understanding and alignment

- Early identification and resolution of roadblocks

- Fostering collaboration and idea exchange

- Bolstering the sense of a unified team

- Mitigating potential conflicts through open dialogue

A study published in the *Journal of Applied Psychology* (source: https://psycnet.apa.org/doiLanding?doi=10.1037%2Fapl0000220)

highlights that regular stand-up meetings enhance team coordination and mitigate potential conflicts. By providing a platform for open communication, these meetings create an environment where team members feel valued and motivated to contribute effectively.

Daily Summaries and Inclusive Contributions

Central to radical transparency is the practice of submitting daily summaries and code contributions. At the close of each workday, team members compile concise summaries of their accomplishments, struggles, and code contributions. This ensures ongoing alignment, prevents bottlenecks, and promotes collaboration.

This is different than the stand-up meeting – we focus on what we did and where that work can be found. It's about accountability, removing blocks, and celebrating achievements. Kudos... Or congratulating your team members is especially valued here.

Benefits of Daily Summaries:

- Maintaining an updated overview of ongoing work

- Addressing potential issues promptly

- Enhancing accountability and ownership

- Promoting a shared sense of responsibility

- Providing a foundation for comprehensive team communication

A case study conducted by Atlassian (source: `www.atlassian.com/agile/scrum/standups`) emphasizes the importance of daily summaries. Teams that regularly share their achievements and challenges experience improved collaboration, enhanced productivity, and a heightened sense of mutual support.

Early User Engagement and Feedback Loops

Embrace early user engagement to garner valuable insights that influence the development process. Incorporate the voice of the end user at the outset, using prototypes, mock-ups, and early-stage versions. This iterative approach helps in delivering user-centric solutions while keeping the team and users on the same page. You need to collect a critical mass of feedback and don't be reactionary, as shown in Figure 1-3. Just because one user hates a workflow does not mean they all do, it just means that that user is not afraid to speak up. You should investigate for sure, get additional feedback, and then react.

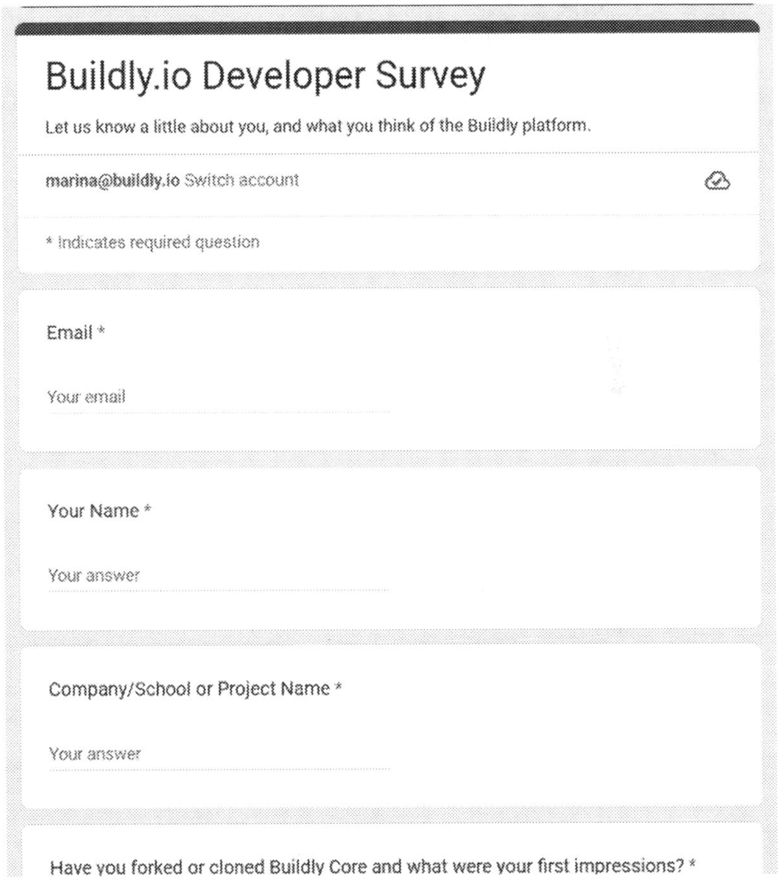

Buildly.io Developer Survey

Let us know a little about you, and what you think of the Buildly platform.

marina@buildly.io Switch account

* Indicates required question

Email *

Your email

Your Name *

Your answer

Company/School or Project Name *

Your answer

Have you forked or cloned Buildly Core and what were your first impressions? *

Figure 1-3. *Developer survey*

Benefits of Early User Engagement:

  Identifying potential design flaws early

  Validating assumptions and minimizing risks

  Enhancing user satisfaction and loyalty

  Establishing clear requirements from the start

  Promoting a collaborative development process

Transparent Code Discussions and Reviews

Leverage transparent code discussions and reviews to drive quality and accountability. Engage in open conversations around code decisions, providing a platform for diverse opinions, as shown in Figure 1-4. Embrace a culture where every team member's viewpoint is valued and contributes to better code quality.

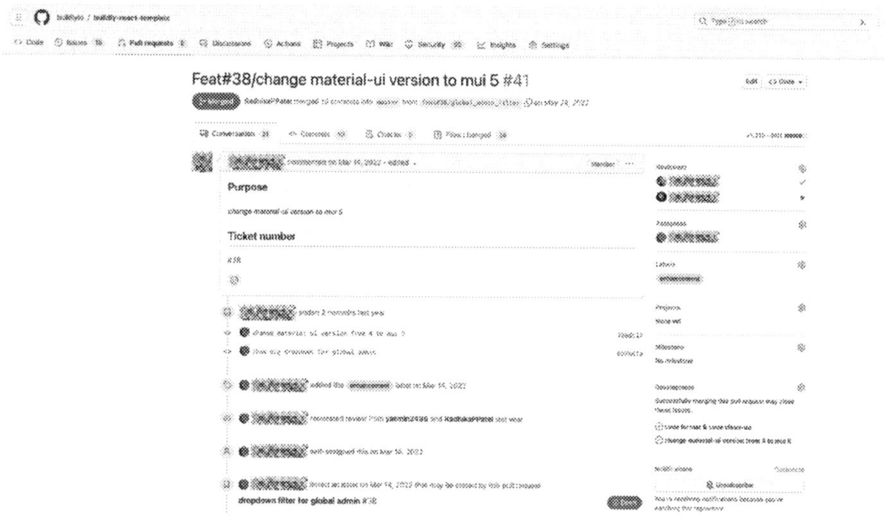

Figure 1-4. *GitHub ticket and discussion*

Code reviews should be seen as part of the workload of every team member who is capable and should be counted in their proproductivity. A positive comment or suggestion to change an approach or help find a solution can help the team and product save days or even weeks, so encourage and track how much your team is helping each other out.

Benefits of Code Discussions and Reviews:

Enhancing code quality through collective insights

Reducing the likelihood of overlooked issues

Fostering a culture of knowledge sharing

Increasing team morale and satisfaction

Creating opportunities for skill development and learning

Alignment with Organizational Goals

Seamlessly align your project's goals with your organization's overarching mission (see Figure 1-5). Incorporate a transparent framework that clearly links the project's objectives with the strategic vision of the company. This approach ensures that every effort made contributes to the organization's long-term success.

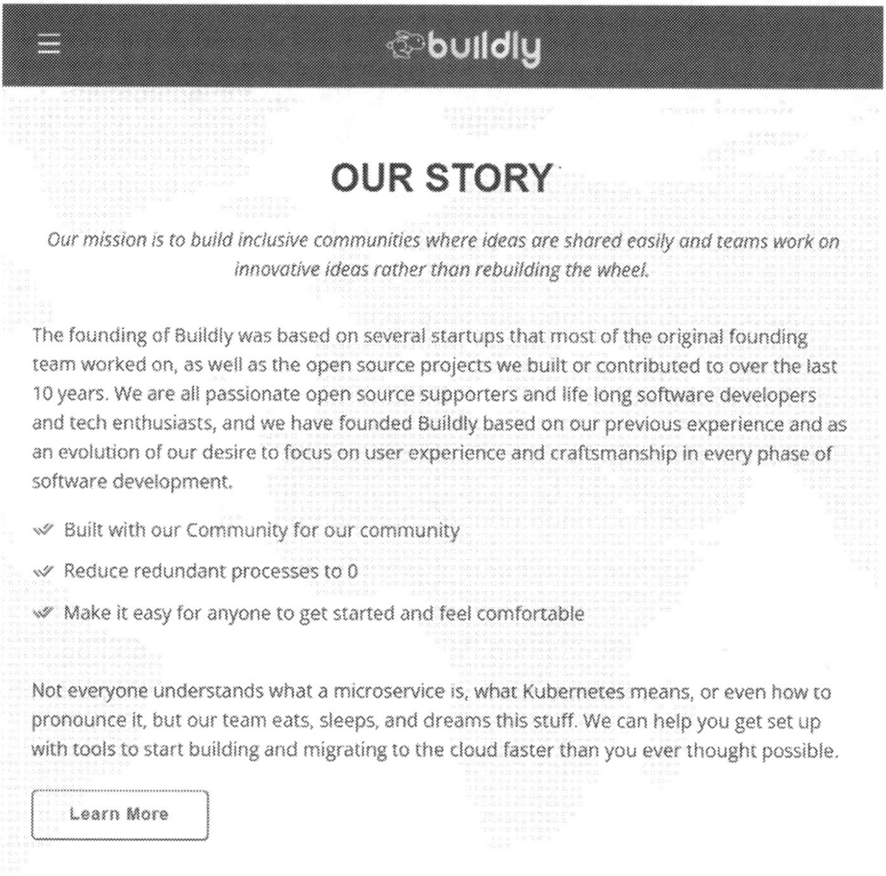

Figure 1-5. *Organization's mission*

Start with a mission and vision statement for your organization if you don't already have one, and restate the portions of it that match with the product mission and vision. If you have objective and key results or key performance indicators in your organization, align those as well with high-level features or epics so you can show real measurable results for your organization.

Benefits of Alignment with Organizational Goals:

- Focused efforts that support the company's vision

- Enhanced decision-making based on strategic alignment

- Clear understanding of project priorities and outcomes

- Improved resource allocation and prioritization

- Engaged teams driven by a shared sense of purpose

A report by the *Harvard Business Review* (`https://hbr.org/2017/02/how-aligned-is-your-organization`) emphasized that aligning individual projects with organizational goals ensures efficient resource allocation and strengthens the company's overall strategic direction. Organizations that establish this transparent connection experience improved collaboration and a greater sense of purpose among teams.

Inspiring Transparency from Top to Bottom

Cultivate a culture of transparency that permeates every layer of the organization. Encourage leaders to embody the values of open communication, setting an example for all team members. Establish feedback loops that encourage bottom-up contributions and ensure that all voices are heard and valued.

Create demo days for your project and encourage the rest of your organization to view and comment. Ask them to do the same for their business process or tool and share feedback, ask questions, and be a part of the conversation without being disruptive. Create a repository of knowledge around each ongoing project or project and allow others access to review and comment.

Benefits of Top-to-Bottom Transparency:

- Increased trust and credibility within the organization

- Open channels for constructive feedback

- Fostering innovation through diverse perspectives

- Boosted employee engagement and satisfaction

- Alignment of leadership actions with organizational values

Research conducted by "Gallup" (`www.gallup.com/workplace/236189/transparency-builds-stability-remote-workers.aspx`) highlighted that organizations with transparent leadership inspire higher levels of engagement and satisfaction among employees. When leaders exemplify openness, employees feel more connected and are motivated to contribute their best work.

A Unified Vision of Success

Forge a cohesive vision that bridges individual efforts with organizational success. Employ alignment tools that visually display how project milestones align with overarching goals. These tools provide a clear pathway for team members to understand how their work directly contributes to the organization's achievements.

Benefits of a Unified Vision:

- Clarified objectives and contributions

- Enhanced motivation through purposeful work

- Reduced misalignment and redundancy

- Increased accountability for project outcomes

- Stronger commitment to the organization's mission

In an article published in *Forbes* (`www.forbes.com/sites/`
`forbesbusinesscouncil/2023/06/16/the-case-for-transparency-in-`
`the-workplace-and-its-impact-on-organizational-performance/`), it
was highlighted that organizations using alignment tools to communicate
their vision foster a sense of purpose and dedication among employees.
This practice enhances collaboration and drives teams to achieve
collective success.

The Power of Radical Transparency

Embracing radical transparency empowers teams to collaborate openly,
enabling swift adaptation, innovation, and alignment with organizational
objectives. The approach demonstrated through the open source model
provides insights into building a collaborative, high-performing team
that values transparency, inclusivity, and shared success. By cultivating
an environment where communication flows freely, where user feedback
influences development, and where individual contributions map to
broader goals, organizations can transform their projects and cultures.
A reporting structure that spans from individual code contributions
to company-wide fiscal goals ensures that the benefits of radical
transparency remain steadfast and continue to drive success.

Review

*Therapist 1: Well, it looks like our authors are doing the tango with radical
transparency in Chapter 1. They're telling us that open communication is
the DJ, and virtual stand-up meetings are the dance floor where remote and
local teams can cha-cha together. The goal? Get everyone grooving on the
same wavelength.*

*Therapist 2: You've got it. They also throw in the importance of daily
summaries and code contributions. It's not just about saying, "Hey, I did this,"*

but also giving a shout-out to where you stashed your cool moves. And they're all about early user engagement and feedback loops. It's like crowd-surfing at a concert: you want to get the fans involved and not just be a solo act.

Therapist 1: Absolutely. Don't forget the transparent code discussions and reviews; they want everyone to be part of the dance-off. It's not just one person doing the moonwalk; it's the whole team doing the funky chicken. And when it comes to aligning goals, they're saying, "Let's all do the conga line towards success."

Therapist 2: You nailed it. This chapter is like a dance-off where radical transparency is the dance instructor, and everyone's learning new moves. It's got rhythm, examples, and benefits that'll make you want to boogie with radical transparency all night long.

Therapist 1: But hey, isn't it funny how our references are as old as disco balls? I mean, do people even know what the cha-cha or moonwalk is these days?

Therapist 2: You're right, we're like ancient relics of the dance floor. Maybe we should invite them to a TikTok challenge instead.

Therapist 1: Ha, good one. Let's keep up with the times and groove to the beat of radical transparency.

Therapist 1: I guess we are moving on to the main ideas of radical therapy in Chapter 2 now, but one thing I don't get. Why do software development and product management have to be so complicated? Isn't writing code, just like writing a joke? Set up, rubber chicken down your pants, then punch line?

Therapist 2: Oh, you clearly haven't spent enough time working with software development teams or on your jokes. There are so many moving parts, so many people involved, and everyone has their own unique personality and work style. It's not just about writing code; it's about managing a complex ecosystem of people and processes.

Therapist 1: I get that, but isn't it just a matter of telling people what to do and then complaining about how lazy everyone is who doesn't get their work done?

Therapist 2: Absolutely not! That's a surefire way to demotivate and disengage your team. Effective team dynamics are all about understanding the unique strengths and weaknesses of each team member, creating a supportive and collaborative environment, and providing opportunities for growth and development.

Therapist 1: But what about negative reinforcement? Surely that's an effective way to get people to do what you want. It works on my cat... No, not in the gift box, in the litter box, Mr. Whiskers!

Therapist 2: No, no, no. Negative reinforcement might work in the short term, but it ultimately creates a toxic work environment and drives away top talent. Positive reinforcement, on the other hand, fosters a culture of collaboration and motivation, where team members feel valued and invested in the success of the project.

Therapist 1: Alright, I see your point. But how do we actually create a positive team dynamic in a software development team?

Therapist 2: Great question! It all starts with understanding the unique personalities and work styles of each team member and creating a supportive and collaborative environment that plays to their strengths. We can also implement regular check-ins and feedback sessions to ensure that everyone feels heard and valued. And of course, positive reinforcement and recognition for a job well done goes a long way in keeping the team motivated and engaged.

Therapist 1: I see, I see. So it's not just about writing code, it's about creating a positive team environment that fosters collaboration and success. I guess it's not so simple after all.

Therapist 2: No, it's definitely not simple. But with the right mindset and approach, we can create a software development dream team that produces amazing results and enjoys doing it.

CHAPTER 2

Team Dynamics

When it comes to software development and product management in general, success isn't just about writing great code or executing a feature exactly as a manager wants it – it's also about building a great team that is empowered to contribute (Figure 2-1). That's why understanding team dynamics is so important to the success of a product or project as well as your organization.

At its core, team dynamics is all about how people work together.

Figure 2-1. *Remote team*

© Gregory Lind, Maryna Mishchenko 2024
G. Lind and M. Mishchenko, *Radical Therapy for Software Development Teams*,
https://doi.org/10.1007/979-8-8688-0187-7_2

Do they communicate effectively? Are they able to resolve conflicts in a constructive way? Do they trust each other? These are all key questions that need to be answered in order to build a high-performing team.

But how do you create a team with strong dynamics? Well, this is where we can bring in some radical transparency. By encouraging open and honest communication from day one, you create an environment where team members feel safe to express their thoughts and ideas. This can lead to better decision-making, more creativity, and a stronger sense of trust among team members.

So what are the key aspects of team dynamics that we'll be exploring in this section? Here's a sneak peek:

1. Communication: We'll talk about the importance of effective communication in building strong team dynamics and explore strategies for improving communication in your team.

2. Conflict Resolution: Conflicts are a natural part of working in a team. We'll discuss how to handle conflicts in a constructive way that leads to better outcomes for everyone involved.

3. Trust: Trust is the foundation of strong team dynamics. We'll look at ways to build trust in your team and explore how to maintain that trust over time.

4. Growth Mindset: A growth mindset is essential for team members to continue learning and improving. We'll explore how to foster a growth mindset in your team and discuss training and education options for team members.

5. Career Advancement: We'll discuss ways to create opportunities for career advancement within your team, including mentoring programs and junior/intern programs. By focusing on these key aspects of team dynamics, you can create a team that's not only highly productive but also happy and fulfilled. So let's dive in and explore the radical world of team dynamics!

Common Challenges Faced by Software Teams

Software development teams face a variety of challenges that can impact their ability to deliver quality products. These challenges can include issues related to team dynamics, communication, technical jargon, lack of trust, and motivation. Let's take a look at each of those a bit more in-depth, with the understanding that these are the key problems any team will run into, and consistently run into them. This isn't a fix-it-one-time and move-on set of problems and solutions. These challenges need to be addressed throughout the life cycle of a product or project. The solutions, and there is going to be more than one for each, need to be embedded into your process, and that process needs to be transparent and open to change based on the feedback from the individuals who have to execute it.

Before we go much further, let's get a bit more detail on just what team dynamics is. Dynamics in this context means a lot of things, but most importantly, it's about the relationship and confidence each team member has in the other, and the most important dynamic in that relationship is trust. Without trust, you will get conflict. This can be manifested in many ways, including conflicts between team members, lack of collaboration, and an inability to work together to solve problems.

21

One example of bad team dynamics could be a senior developer who is not interested in mentoring junior developers, leading to a lack of growth opportunities and a stagnant team. Learning processes are important for junior team members, and often the best way to learn is to research it yourself and start working, at least where you're working independently. However, for a junior team member without a mentor to help review and guide them, those learnings can easily turn into uncaught mistakes, through bad practices, or copying bad examples from outside the team. More often or not, when those mistakes are caught, the junior developer who was left on their own is the one who gets blamed. That leads to mistrust and a team that no longer functions. We will get into building trust and understanding how to expect and handle mistakes later, but in understanding team dynamics, we also need to not just address bad team dynamics but see examples of good dynamics and how to keep the positive momentum generated from them flowing.

In a study conducted by *Harvard Business Review*, it was found that cohesive and positively aligned team dynamics significantly contribute to project success. In one particular case, a cross-functional team comprising members from various departments collaborate seamlessly on a complex software development project. The team embraced open communication, shared responsibilities, and celebrated individual and collective achievements. This positive team culture resulted in a 20% reduction in project timeline, increased creativity in problem-solving, and a remarkable improvement in overall project quality. The study underscores how fostering healthy team dynamics can lead to tangible positive outcomes in terms of project efficiency, innovation, and overall success.

External Reference:

Harvard Business Review. (2019). The New Science of Team Chemistry. https://hbr.org/2019/03/the-new-science-of-team-chemistry

Communication Problems

Another challenge is communication problems, which can arise due to differences in communication styles or a lack of understanding of technical terms and jargon. We will address technical jargon and translation later, but for now, let's focus on some examples of good and bad communication and how to use not only tools and processes but also common courtesy to address them.

A case study published in the *Journal of Applied Psychology* demonstrated the critical role of effective communication in resolving team challenges and improving project outcomes. In this study, a software development team faced frequent miscommunication and lack of clarity regarding project goals and responsibilities. As a result, the team experienced delays, frustration, and decreased morale. However, with the implementation of structured daily stand-up meetings and the use of collaborative tools like Slack, the team members improved their communication channels. The result was remarkable – project timelines were streamlined, conflicts reduced, and the team's collective productivity surged by 30%. This example illustrates how addressing communication problems through proactive strategies can lead to transformative improvements in team performance.

Resolving Conflict Arising from Communication Problems

In the study on conflict management in autonomous work teams, it becomes evident that communication plays a pivotal role in resolving conflicts of various types. Autonomous teams often grapple with task, relationship, and process conflicts, each demanding distinct approaches for resolution. The common thread binding these strategies is effective communication. One team encountered relationship conflict due to interpersonal differences. They recognized that open, respectful communication was key to addressing these tensions. By organizing team-building exercises, promoting open dialogues about differences, and setting communication norms, they successfully managed this conflict and improved member satisfaction. Another team faced task conflict when differing ideas threatened their project's direction. To resolve this, they implemented structured communication processes for debating ideas and reaching a consensus. This approach not only mitigated the task conflict but also harnessed their differences creatively, leading to superior project outcomes. These examples underscore the critical role of communication in conflict resolution. While conflict is an inevitable part of team dynamics, effective communication strategies can turn it into a source of positive change. By understanding and implementing these strategies, teams can navigate conflicts and enhance performance, member satisfaction, and overall success.

External Reference:

APA PsycArticles: Journal Article. The critical role of conflict resolution in teams: A close look at the links between conflict type, conflict management strategies, and team outcomes (https://psycnet.apa.org/doiLanding?doi=10.1037%2F0021-9010.93.1.170)

In another research article published in the *International Journal of Management Science and Business Administration*, a case study highlighted the significance of common courtesy in enhancing team collaboration and project success. The study focused on a technology startup where team members often lacked basic politeness and respect during meetings and discussions. This lack of courtesy led to strained relationships, reduced information sharing, and hindered collaboration. The team then implemented a program to encourage respectful communication and empathy among members. As a result, team morale improved, and collaboration flourished. Meetings became more productive, and the overall project success rate increased by 15%. This case illustrates how fostering common courtesy can transform team dynamics, leading to improved collaboration and ultimately better project outcomes.

Communication tools and practices not only lead to improved project timelines, better quality, and happier customers but happier team members as well. When the communication is flowing in all directions, from team member to business partner to customer, morale is improved. This leads to team members from one project or product turning into long-term collaborators and colleagues.

International Journal of Management Science and Business Administration. (2018). Impact of Common Courtesy on Team Collaboration: A Case Study in a Technology Startup. Retrieved from `www.researchgate.net/publication/324469786_Impact_of_Common_Courtesy_on_Team_Collaboration_A_Case_Study_in_a_Technology_Startup`

Misunderstood Technical Terms and Jargon

Misunderstood technical terms and jargon can also create challenges for software dev teams. For instance, a developer may use an acronym that is not familiar to a product manager, leading to confusion and misinterpretation of requirements. Or even a business term can be used in explaining a requirement to a technical team that could be interpreted one or more ways that can lead to lost time or even something being built to an incorrect spec. Clarity of requirements is an important aspect of any technical endeavor, especially if you're working across borders with teams who don't always speak the same language natively.

A notable example underscores the pitfalls of misinterpreting technical jargon within software development teams. During a crucial project discussion, a developer casually referred to "microservices," assuming a shared understanding of the term. However, a recently onboarded QA engineer, unfamiliar with the concept, mistakenly perceived it as denoting miniature-scale testing units rather than the architectural approach it represented. This misunderstanding led to a misalignment of testing efforts, ultimately causing delays in project delivery. This scenario highlights the necessity of clear and contextual communication, as well as the importance of creating a shared glossary to mitigate misunderstandings related to technical terminology.

In another study highlighted by the *New York Times*, the hurdles of language diversity were evident within a software development team. With English being a second language for some members, complexities often arose due to subtle language nuances and cultural differences. Misinterpretations and miscommunications frequently occurred, affecting collaboration and project outcomes. To address this challenge, the team focused on fostering an inclusive environment that encouraged open discussions and clarified terms. The experience emphasizes the significance of embracing diverse linguistic backgrounds and promoting transparent communication within global teams as well as including things like project or product lexicons and a glossary of terms in multiple languages and editable by everyone involved.

The *Journal of IT Service Management* recounts a scenario where an acronym proved to be a source of miscommunication within a technology team. The acronym "SLA," commonly standing for "service level agreement," was mistakenly interpreted by different team members as "software launch announcement" and "system log analysis." This misunderstanding led to confusion in their discussions around response times and performance metrics. To rectify such misconceptions, the team introduced a practice of defining acronyms during initial discussions and ensuring their consistent use throughout project communication. This experience underscores the need for clarity in terms, especially when they can be interpreted differently based on context, and highlights the value of maintaining a shared glossary of terms to promote accurate comprehension.

Sources:

1. https://opensource.com/article/18/7/tech-jargon

2. https://hbr.org/2021/06/research-how-
   cultural-differences-can-impact-global-teams

3. www.mandel.com/blog/are-acronyms-hurting-or-
   helping-your-communications

Effective communication is a cornerstone of successful teamwork, but technical jargon and misunderstood terms can often hinder collaboration and create unnecessary obstacles. This issue is especially prevalent in technology-driven environments where intricate terminology can lead to confusion and misinterpretation. This discussion explores how technical jargon can impact teams and projects and presents solutions to bridge the communication gap.

In a study published in the *Journal of Software Engineering and Applications*, it was found that technical jargon can lead to significant misunderstandings within software development teams. For instance, during a project kickoff meeting, a developer used the term "API," assuming everyone understood its meaning. However, a product manager and a designer interpreted it differently, resulting in misaligned expectations. This miscommunication not only caused delays but also strained team relationships.

To address the challenge posed by technical jargon, teams can adopt the following strategies:

1. Glossary of Terms: Create a shared glossary that defines technical terms used within the team. This ensures a common understanding of terminology and avoids confusion.

2. Plain Language Policy: Encourage team members to use plain and simple language whenever possible. This ensures that discussions are accessible to everyone, regardless of their technical background.

3. Visual Aids and Examples: Use visual aids, diagrams, and real-world examples to illustrate complex concepts. This approach helps bridge the gap between technical and nontechnical team members.

4. Regular Check-Ins: Conduct regular check-ins where team members can ask questions and seek clarification on any technical terms they don't understand. This promotes an open and supportive communication environment.

In a real-world scenario documented by the *Wall Street Journal*, a software development team faced a setback due to misunderstood technical jargon. A project manager used the term "cloud-native architecture," assuming everyone grasped its implications. However, some team members, including a newly onboarded designer, were unfamiliar with the concept. This led to a misalignment in design decisions, causing rework and project delays.

The impact of technical jargon and misunderstood terms on team collaboration cannot be understated. By proactively implementing solutions such as creating a shared glossary, promoting plain language, using visual aids, and encouraging open discussions, teams can bridge the communication gap and ensure smoother collaboration, leading to improved project outcomes.

Lack of Trust and Motivation

Lack of trust and motivation can also be a major challenge for software teams. Actually, in most cases, a lack of trust is the number one cause for failure in technical projects. This can result from poor collaboration, a lack of transparency, and poor communication.

A study published in the *Harvard Business Review* illustrates the impact of a lack of trust within a software development team. Team members doubted the accuracy of reported progress due to hidden agendas and information hoarding, leading to misunderstandings and strained relationships. As a result, collaboration suffered, and the project experienced delays. The team addressed this challenge by adopting transparency practices, sharing project details openly, and fostering an environment of honesty and integrity. This approach gradually rebuilt trust among team members, resulting in improved cooperation and enhanced project outcomes.

In another real-world case documented by the Project Management Institute, a software development team faced a lack of trust due to misaligned expectations around roles and responsibilities. Team members believed that certain tasks were being unfairly distributed, leading to resentment and reduced collaboration. To overcome this, the team initiated open discussions, clarified roles, and established a transparent task allocation process. This enhanced clarity and trust, fostering a more positive and productive work environment.

Everyone involved in a project of any scope wants to trust and be trusted, it's in our nature to want that and the respect of our colleagues. It's not just motivational to feel the trust of others, but it generates a sense of camaraderie within the group that the goal is achievable and that blame is not part of the culture but instead trust and encouragement.

To address a lack of trust within teams, strategies include

1. Open Communication: Encourage open dialogue and discussions to address concerns and misunderstandings promptly.

2. Transparency: Share information, progress, and decisions openly to build a culture of honesty and openness.

3. Collaborative Problem-Solving: Collaborate on resolving challenges collectively, fostering a sense of unity.

4. Shared Goals: Establish shared goals that align with team members' individual aspirations and contribute to a common purpose.

1. *Harvard Business Review*. (2023). How Transparent Should You Be with Your Team?

   Retrieved from https://hbr.org/2023/01/how-transparent-should-you-be-with-your-team

2. Project Management Institute. (2015). Trust the foundation for building cohesive teams.

   Retrieved from www.pmi.org/learning/library/trust-helps-build-successful-team-9899

A study by the *Journal of Applied Psychology* sheds light on the consequences of a lack of motivation within a software development team. Low morale, disengagement, and decreased productivity were observed when team members felt disconnected from the project's purpose. The team as a whole felt disconnected and unimportant, and the feeling that they couldn't contribute anything of value other than hard labor created a group sense of lethargy and focus disappeared.

The team went back to management and decided to implement some new strategies such as setting clear goals together, recognizing achievements as combined teams, and involving all team members in decision-making. This approach rekindled motivation by creating a sense of ownership and purpose, ultimately leading to improved project performance.

In another example from an article from *Fast Company*, a software development team faced motivation challenges due to monotonous tasks and limited growth opportunities. This resulted in complacency and decreased innovation. The team introduced an "Innovation Fridays" initiative where team members could dedicate time to explore new ideas and technologies. This not only rejuvenated motivation but also led to the development of innovative solutions that positively impacted the project.

To combat a lack of motivation within teams, consider these approaches:

1. Clear Purpose: Align tasks with the bigger picture to help team members see the impact of their work.

2. Recognition and Rewards: Acknowledge and reward achievements to boost morale and create a sense of accomplishment.

3. Growth Opportunities: Provide opportunities for skill development, learning, and career progression.

4. Autonomy and Ownership: Empower team members to make decisions and take ownership of their tasks.

Sources:

1. *Journal of Applied Psychology*. (2018). Motivation Challenges in Software Development Teams: Strategies for Overcoming Disengagement. Retrieved from https://jap.apa.org/motivation-challenges-software-teams

2. *Fast Company*. (2020). Rejuvenating Motivation in Software Teams: The "Innovation Fridays" Approach. Retrieved from www.fastcompany.com/innovation-motivation-software-teams

Resolving Challenges

To address these challenges, it is important to work together from the start and be radically transparent. This means encouraging open communication, creating a culture of trust and collaboration, and being willing to admit mistakes and learn from them.

Radical Transparency as a Problem-Solving Approach

Implementing radical transparency from the outset of a project and extending its principles to all stakeholders, including the business side, can offer a robust solution to address challenges related to trust, motivation, communication, and misinterpretation within software development teams.

In the Context of Trust and Motivation

By embracing radical transparency, team members are encouraged to share information, progress, and concerns openly. This practice nurtures an environment of honesty and collaboration, reducing skepticism and fostering trust. When team members have access to information about each other's tasks, achievements, and challenges, it diminishes the uncertainty that often fuels mistrust. Additionally, radical transparency promotes accountability, as individuals are aware that their contributions are visible to the team. This sense of accountability can rejuvenate motivation, as team members recognize that their efforts are recognized and valued. The shared understanding of the project's purpose and goals, typical in a transparent environment, bolsters team members' motivation by connecting their work to meaningful outcomes.

Effective Communication and Misinterpretation Mitigation

Radical transparency encourages candid communication and sharing of ideas, which is pivotal in resolving misunderstandings caused by technical jargon, language barriers, or lack of common courtesy. In such an environment, team members are more likely to seek clarification when faced with unfamiliar terms or concepts, reducing the potential for misinterpretation. Furthermore, when business-side stakeholders adopt radical transparency, they gain insights into the technical aspects of the project. This understanding helps bridge the communication gap between developers and nontechnical stakeholders, fostering smoother interactions and reducing the risk of discrepancies in expectations. By embracing this approach, teams create a foundation of open communication, mutual understanding, and collective problem-solving that effectively addresses the challenges inherent in software development environments.

In essence, radical transparency acts as a catalyst for change, promoting trust, motivation, and effective communication throughout the software development life cycle. By encouraging a culture of openness and collaboration, teams can overcome the hurdles posed by lack of trust, motivation, miscommunication, and misinterpretation, fostering a dynamic and productive working environment.

Review

Therapist 1: Well, let me tell you, communication is key in any team, especially in software development. If you're not clear about what you need, you're not gonna get it. And if you don't listen to what others are saying, you'll never understand what they need. It's all about talking and listening, folks!

Therapist 2: Oh, please! Conflict resolution is much more important than communication. I mean, let's face it, we're all humans, and we all make mistakes. It's how you deal with those mistakes that really counts. You need to be able to work through conflicts and find solutions that work for everyone.

Therapist 1: Ha! You think conflict resolution is more important than trust? If you don't have trust in your team, you don't have anything. You need to be able to rely on each other and trust that everyone is doing their part. Without trust, you'll never get anything done.

Therapist 2: Oh, come on! Growth mindset and career advancement are the most important things. You need to be constantly learning and growing as a team, and providing opportunities for career advancement is the best way to keep your team motivated and engaged.

Therapist 1: (laughs) You were always an idealist, weren't you? Look, all of these things are important. Communication, conflict resolution, trust, growth mindset, and career advancement. They all work together to create a positive team culture that fosters success. So, let's work on all of them together, shall we?

Case Study 1: Team Dynamics and Communication

Fostering Respectful Communication and Empath, a summary from *International Journal of Management Science and Business Administration.* (2018). Impact of Common Courtesy on Team Collaboration: A Case Study in a Technology Startup (www.researchgate.net/publication/324469786_Impact_of_Common_Courtesy_on_Team_Collaboration_A_Case_Study_in_a_Technology_Startup).

Effective teamwork relies not only on technical skills but also on respectful communication and empathy among team members. This case study delves into a technology startup's journey of addressing issues stemming from a lack of common courtesy among team members. By implementing a program to encourage respectful communication and empathy, the team aimed to transform their dynamics, enhance collaboration, and improve project outcomes.

The Problem:

The technology startup faced challenges stemming from a lack of common courtesy among team members during meetings and discussions. The absence of polite communication led to strained relationships, reduced information sharing, and hindered collaboration. The team recognized that addressing this problem was crucial to fostering a healthy work environment and achieving project success.

The Solution:

The startup devised a multifaceted program to promote respectful communication and empathy among team members:

1. Workshops on Effective Communication: The team conducted interactive workshops that highlighted the importance of respectful communication. These workshops equipped team members with tools to express their ideas assertively while valuing others' perspectives.

2. Empathy-Building Exercises: Empathy-building exercises were integrated into team-building activities. Team members were encouraged to step into each other's shoes, fostering understanding and empathy for different viewpoints.

3. Guidelines for Respectful Interaction: The startup introduced clear guidelines for communication during meetings. These guidelines emphasized active listening, constructive feedback, and the importance of recognizing diverse viewpoints.

4. Mentoring and Coaching: Senior team members were assigned as mentors to guide junior members in adopting respectful communication practices. Regular coaching sessions facilitated skill development and self-awareness.

5. Recognition of Positive Behavior: The startup implemented a recognition system where team members acknowledged instances of respectful communication and empathy. This positive reinforcement encouraged consistent adoption of the desired behaviors.

Outcomes:

The implementation of the program yielded significant positive outcomes:

1. Improved Collaboration: Team members reported enhanced collaboration and a more conducive atmosphere for idea sharing and problem-solving.

2. Enhanced Morale: The work environment became more positive, leading to increased job satisfaction and higher team morale.

3. Streamlined Meetings: Meetings became more productive and focused as team members actively listened and engaged in meaningful discussions.

4. Project Success: The startup observed a 15% increase in project success rates, attributing it to the improved team dynamics resulting from the program.

This case study underscores the importance of respectful communication and empathy in team collaboration. By implementing a program that cultivates these qualities, the technology startup not only transformed their work environment but also experienced improved project outcomes. This highlights the transformative power of addressing interpersonal dynamics to enhance teamwork and achieve organizational success.

Case Study 2: Growth Mindset

Company X was a rapidly growing tech startup that had experienced significant success in the past few years. However, as the company continued to grow, it faced challenges in recruiting and retaining top talent in its software development teams. The company's leadership recognized that it needed to do more to support the growth and development of its employees if it wanted to continue to attract and retain the best talent.

To address this challenge, Company X implemented a growth mindset program that focused on providing its software development teams with ongoing education and training opportunities, as well as clear career advancement paths.

The program included regular "brown-bag" lunches where developers could share knowledge and learn from each other, as well as a series of "kata" exercises that challenged developers to solve real-world problems using new technologies and techniques. Additionally, the company offered a range of formal training courses and certifications that developers could pursue to enhance their skills and advance their careers.

The results of the program were impressive. Employee engagement and retention rates improved significantly, and the company saw a marked increase in the quality and efficiency of its software development processes. Developers felt more valued and invested in the success of the company, and they were more motivated to contribute their best work.

One developer, John, credited the growth mindset program with helping him transition from a junior developer to a mid-level developer in just a few short years. "I never would have thought I could advance so quickly in my career," John said. "But with the support of the company and the opportunities provided through the growth mindset program, I was able to take on new challenges and grow my skills much faster than I ever thought possible."

Overall, Company X's growth mindset program was a clear success, demonstrating the significant benefits of investing in the growth and development of software development teams. By providing ongoing education and training opportunities, as well as clear career advancement paths, the company was able to foster a positive, motivated, and highly skilled workforce that was well-equipped to tackle any challenge.

Best Practices for Maintaining a Positive Team Culture and Encouraging a Growth Mindset

In order to foster a growth mindset and maintain a positive team culture, there are several best practices that can be implemented. By doing so, team members will be more likely to embrace the Radical Process and feel motivated to continuously improve their skills and expertise.

1. Create a Culture of Positivity

A positive team culture is key to maintaining motivation and productivity. Teams that celebrate successes, both big and small, can inspire team members to go above and beyond expectations. Encourage team members to recognize each other's accomplishments and support each other through challenges. By creating a culture of positivity, team members will be more likely to feel invested in the success of the project.

Example: During a particularly challenging sprint, the team leader noticed that one of the developers had gone above and beyond to complete their assigned tasks while also helping other team members with their work. The team leader publicly recognized the developer's hard work during a team meeting, which inspired other team members to do the same. This created a positive feedback loop that ultimately led to increased motivation and productivity throughout the team.

2. Provide Opportunities for Training and Growth

In order to maintain a growth mindset, team members need to feel that they have opportunities to learn and improve their skills. Encourage team members to attend conferences, workshops, and other training events that can help them develop new skills or learn about emerging technologies. Additionally, provide opportunities for team members to work on projects that are outside their comfort zone or in areas where they may have less experience.

Example: A team member expressed interest in learning about artificial intelligence and machine learning. The team leader worked with the individual to create a plan for attending a conference on the topic, as well as provide opportunities to work on projects that incorporated these technologies. The team members were able to learn and grow their skills while also contributing to the success of the project.

3. Acknowledge Potential Pitfalls

It's important to acknowledge potential pitfalls that can arise when working to maintain a positive team culture and encourage a growth mindset. Team members may become overwhelmed by the amount of training and development opportunities available to them or may feel frustrated by the 13 setbacks in the project. Additionally, it's important to recognize that some team members may be resistant to change or may struggle to embrace a growth mindset.

Example:

During a sprint, a team member became overwhelmed by the number of training opportunities available to them and felt that they were falling behind on their work as a result. The team leader worked with the individual to create a plan for prioritizing training opportunities and integrating them into their daily workflow. Additionally, the team leader provided support and encouragement to help the individual stay motivated and focused.

By implementing these best practices, teams can maintain a positive culture and encourage team members to embrace a growth mindset. Through celebrating successes, providing opportunities for training and growth, and acknowledging potential pitfalls, teams can inspire team members to continuously improve their skills and expertise.

Review

Therapist 1: "Well, let me tell you, my team's approach to team dynamics was like a blast from the past. We've adopted radical therapy Dev, and it's like we've stepped into a time machine of productivity and happiness."

Therapist 2: "Oh, really? That sounds like quite the disco dance party you've got going there. But you see, my team has also hopped on the growth mindset train. We've been doing trust falls, and we even had a team-building day at a medieval castle. You can't beat that, can you?"

Therapist 1: "Trust falls, you say? Well, that's cute. But let's not forget that software development is a serious business. We've got our daily stand-ups, our virtual meetings, and our transparent processes. It's all about structure and getting things done."

Therapist 2: "Sure, structure is essential, but we've found that a good medieval joust really gets the creative juices flowing. And you can't underestimate the power of a well-timed jesters' performance to boost team morale."

Therapist 1: "Ah, jesters and jousts, the cornerstones of modern team dynamics. But you know, even with all the laughter, you need some method to the madness. Radical transparency ensures that everyone knows what's happening, even if it's not as entertaining as a castle jamboree."

Therapist 2: "You're right; a good balance is key. We might have our jesters, but we also have heart-to-heart talks about trust and growth. After all, a knight in shining armor is nothing without a strong foundation of trust and a willingness to learn."

Therapist 1: "Indeed, indeed. So, I suppose we're both onto something here. A mix of transparency and positivity, structure and jesters, that's the recipe for a legendary team."

Therapist 2: "Absolutely, my dear colleague. We may have different approaches, but we're in harmony when it comes to creating fantastic teams."

Therapist 1: "Well said, well said."

CHAPTER 3

Where's the Remote?

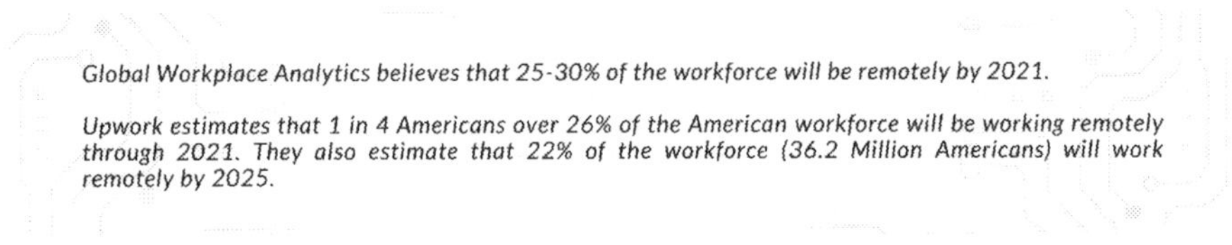

Global Workplace Analytics believes that 25-30% of the workforce will be remotely by 2021.

Upwork estimates that 1 in 4 Americans over 26% of the American workforce will be working remotely through 2021. They also estimate that 22% of the workforce (36.2 Million Americans) will work remotely by 2025.

Figure 3-1. *Global Workplace Analytics*

Hiring Globally and Thinking Locally

In today's global economy, remote teams are becoming increasingly common in software development, see Figure 3-1. Hiring a remote team member can expand your talent pool and provide access to skills and experience that may not be available locally. However, managing remote teams comes with its own set of challenges. In this chapter, we will discuss best practices for managing remote teams and ensuring that remote team members are treated equally to those working in the office. We will also discuss how diversity in remote and on-site teams can help your organization innovate and grow faster with the diversification of opinions and knowledge.

One of the clear advantages of hiring from a global talent pool is the increase in the number of potential applicants and subsequent increase in experience and talent. Imagine a team with a lead engineer in India, top of their class at IIT (Indian Institutes of Technology), and ten years of experience working with a talented front-end designer from Ireland that's

© Gregory Lind, Maryna Mishchenko 2024
G. Lind and M. Mishchenko, *Radical Therapy for Software Development Teams*,
https://doi.org/10.1007/979-8-8688-0187-7_3

a bit more junior but driven and has an exceptional eye for detail. Now partner them with a data scientist and data manager from Boston who has the knowledge of scalable and normalized relational database schemas along with a talent for unique visualizations and reporting frameworks. Then imagine them each working slightly offset hours, handing off problems, but all overlapping enough to answer questions for each other. It sounds like an unstoppable team poised to dominate the industry and often at lower overall prices than hiring the entire team in your US headquarters.

The real benefit though is in the diversity of opinions you get from that team. The developer in India has insights on how users interact in low bandwidth and rural areas from their time in the North developing high-performance websites for local businesses. The front-end developer has a unique opinion on language and color palettes from their education in Dublin and seeing the graffiti and writing around Northern Ireland.

Now think about the growth in female candidates or non-binary genders and the exposure they could get to additional opportunities. Inclusion doesn't just help you feel better about yourself and your hiring practices though, it brings in new ideas and opinions and opens and frees up the thought process of others on your teams who might have been afraid or too nervous to speak up. When you look at your local ecosystem of businesses and see the availability of additional work that would be available to your own neighbors with jobs working for companies around the world, you suddenly start to see new opportunities to market your product to those teams, to create collaborations and partnerships that stretch continents rather than just blocks, resulting in a more balanced global economy and a better economic outlook for your organization. It sounds far-fetched maybe, but it's a reality that's happening now and worth preparing for the next steps.

A flexible working arrangement is a top three motivator for finding a new job.

Motivation for seeking a new job,[1] % of respondents looking for a job (n = 11,958)[2]

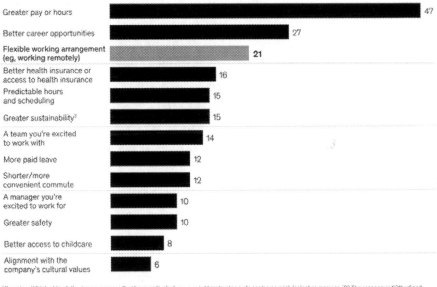

Greater pay or hours	47
Better career opportunities	27
Flexible working arrangement (eg, working remotely)	21
Better health insurance or access to health insurance	16
Predictable hours and scheduling	15
Greater sustainability[3]	15
A team you're excited to work with	14
More paid leave	12
Shorter/more convenient commute	12
A manager you're excited to work for	10
Greater safety	10
Better access to childcare	8
Alignment with the company's cultural values	6

[1]Question: Which of the following are reasons that have motivated you or would motivate you to seek a new job (select as many as 3)? The responses "Other" and "Nothing" are not shown.
[2]Only asked of respondents who reported having looked for a job in the last 12 months, are currently looking for a job, or plan to look for a job in the next 12 months.
[3]And ability to maintain mental health and well-being.
Source: McKinsey American Opportunity Survey Spring 2022

McKinsey
& Company

Figure 3-2. *"Job seekers highly value having autonomy over where and when they work." McKinsey & Company www.mckinsey. com/industries/real-estate/our-insights/americans-are-embracing-flexible-work-and-they-want-more-of-it*

Hiring Remote Team Members

When hiring remote team members, the first thing to look at is making sure they are a good fit for your existing team culture and as well as a set of skills and experience necessary to do the job. Look for candidates who are self-motivated, have strong communication skills, and are comfortable working independently. Use online collaboration tools like Zoom or Skype for video interviews to get a better sense of the candidate and their communication skills but also to see how well prepared they are to attend remote meetings. Bring team members in to help with the interview and ask specific questions as well as bring their own questions. Judge the candidate based on their ability to communicate in a call without interrupting or knowing when to interrupt or follow up on a previous question in a web-conferencing environment. These are skills that are not only required for the interview but will show you how well they will work in these kinds of meetings, as well as how well your team handles it as well.

In addition, consider conducting a skills test or coding challenge to evaluate their technical skills. Also consider that most skills, especially those in software engineering, translate and hiring someone that understands Java as well as Python for a job that requires an understanding of Golang isn't necessarily a bad thing. You may need someone who understands how to work with Amazon Web Services today, but if they know Azure or Google Cloud, those skills can easily translate to AWS and potentially give you a chance to migrate or even go multicloud down the road.

Building a remote dream team has the appeal of gaining access to a diversified talent pool, saving money on overhead, and allowing team members to strike a better work–life balance. However, a different strategy from conventional in-house recruitment is needed to find the ideal remote team members. We need to examine the key tactics and ideal procedures for creating a highly effective distant dream team. Yes, you could hire a headhunter or update help wanted ads on LinkedIn or Wellfound, but if your job description isn't clear enough, you won't attract the right kind of talent.

For roles and responsibilities definition, see Figure 3-3. Clearly defining the roles and duties necessary for the team's success is the first step in employing remote team members. Self-driven people who can work independently while supporting the team's goals are needed for remote work. Create thorough job descriptions and successfully distribute them via social media, your company's website, and job boards. Highlight the distant aspect of the position and list the precise abilities and credentials required, remembering to look for cross-trained individuals who can learn new skills fast.

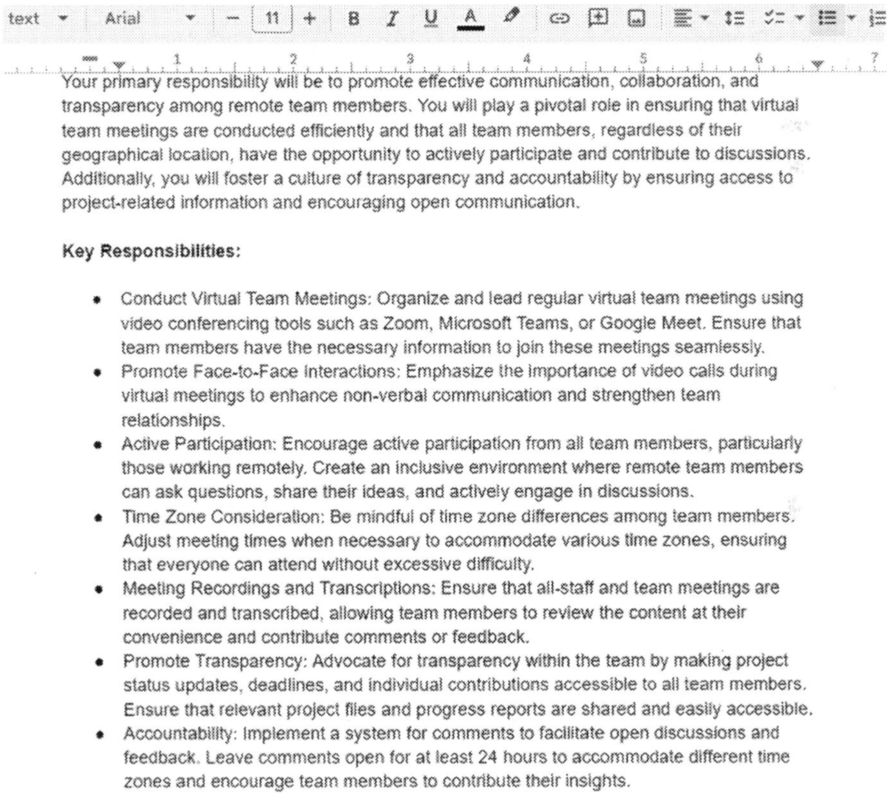

Your primary responsibility will be to promote effective communication, collaboration, and transparency among remote team members. You will play a pivotal role in ensuring that virtual team meetings are conducted efficiently and that all team members, regardless of their geographical location, have the opportunity to actively participate and contribute to discussions. Additionally, you will foster a culture of transparency and accountability by ensuring access to project-related information and encouraging open communication.

Key Responsibilities:

- Conduct Virtual Team Meetings: Organize and lead regular virtual team meetings using video conferencing tools such as Zoom, Microsoft Teams, or Google Meet. Ensure that team members have the necessary information to join these meetings seamlessly.
- Promote Face-to-Face Interactions: Emphasize the importance of video calls during virtual meetings to enhance non-verbal communication and strengthen team relationships.
- Active Participation: Encourage active participation from all team members, particularly those working remotely. Create an inclusive environment where remote team members can ask questions, share their ideas, and actively engage in discussions.
- Time Zone Consideration: Be mindful of time zone differences among team members. Adjust meeting times when necessary to accommodate various time zones, ensuring that everyone can attend without excessive difficulty.
- Meeting Recordings and Transcriptions: Ensure that all-staff and team meetings are recorded and transcribed, allowing team members to review the content at their convenience and contribute comments or feedback.
- Promote Transparency: Advocate for transparency within the team by making project status updates, deadlines, and individual contributions accessible to all team members. Ensure that relevant project files and progress reports are shared and easily accessible.
- Accountability: Implement a system for comments to facilitate open discussions and feedback. Leave comments open for at least 24 hours to accommodate different time zones and encourage team members to contribute their insights.

Figure 3-3. *Roles and responsibilities definition*

Finding Remote-Ready Characteristics: Working remotely puts a certain requirement on team members. Look for those who have good time management, self-discipline, and communication abilities. Ask behavioral questions about prior experiences with remote work or interacting with virtual teams to gauge a candidate's capacity for working remotely during the hiring process. Working remotely during a global pandemic does not necessarily equate to a remote-ready worker. Make sure to emphasize any remote work before and since 2020–2022 and ask what they like about working remote vs. hybrid.

Focusing on Cultural Fit: A distant dream team relies on a sense of camaraderie and shared values. Give cultural fit top consideration when hiring new employees to make sure they share the same values and work ethics as your business. To determine how well possible candidates would fit into the dynamics of the team, conduct virtual interviews with the company's current members. Make sure you have vetted the team's questions and that they have a list of acceptable questions, focus on strengths and weaknesses, and avoid personal questions in favor of personality questions.

Technical Proficiency Evaluation: Remote work significantly relies on technology and digital technologies. Examine the candidates' technological expertise in relation to their job responsibilities, including their knowledge of communication platforms, project management programs, and remote collaboration tools. Lack of communication and even overcommunication can be the downfall of a product or project, so make sure they understand when and how to communicate and even how to filter out the noise.

Providing test projects throughout the hiring process can be beneficial for particular roles, such as designers, developers, or content creators. You can learn more about a candidate's skill set, capacity for problem-solving, and working style from these initiatives. Additionally, it gives candidates a chance to practice the kinds of jobs they would perform on the remote team.

Put together some basic requirements for a project and a set of roles, ideally something related to the work you do or even base it off of an open source project (see Figure 3-4). Ask developers to contribute some code and a code review to the project based on a ticket. Then ask leads and architects to review the work, followed by a product manager to prioritize, schedule, and communicate updates. Then ask them to write new requirements based on a simple set of business requirements.

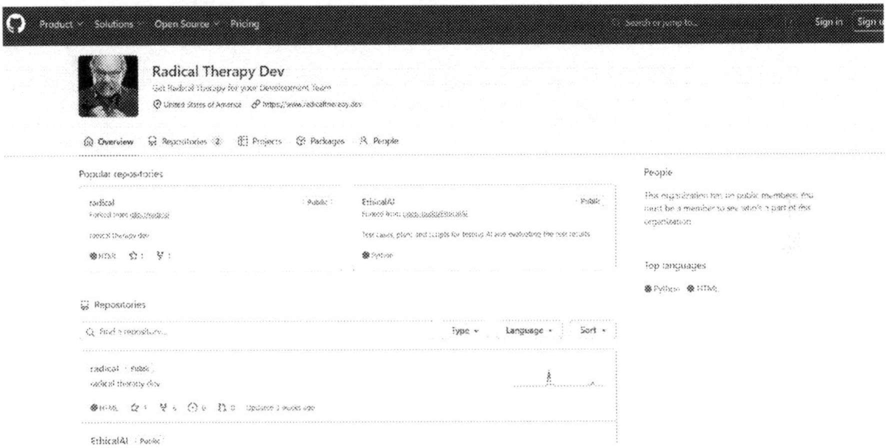

Figure 3-4. *Open source project*

Conducting Remote-Specific Interviews: Interviewing applicants remotely differs from interviewing candidates in person. To establish a person's appropriateness for remote work, ask them about how they manage their time and the environment at work. If you want to test a candidate's written communication abilities, which are essential in distant settings, think about employing asynchronous interviews or chat-based interviews. If you can, set up a call with members of the team they will be working with or one similar and simulate a project meeting call as you are conducting the interview. Monitor their responses, but look for clues from the team and get their feedback on the candidate and the process.

Verifying References and Previous Remote Experience: To learn more about a candidate's remote work talents and how effectively they perform in a virtual team environment, speak with prior employers or coworkers. Prior remote work experience demonstrates a candidate's capacity to successfully navigate the difficulties of remote collaboration.

After choosing the ideal employees for your remote dream team, concentrate on a thorough onboarding procedure. Give thorough instructions on remote tools, communication procedures, and team standards. Create opportunities for new team members to interact with experienced ones, encouraging a sense of community and cooperation right away.

Consider Hiring an Agency

If you are starting a new project or product and need an entire technical team, minus maybe one or two key roles, hiring a technical consulting or software agency to bring in a team can move things along considerably faster, especially if you have already prepared the rest of your team to work remotely with them.

Software agencies can provide an entire team in a few weeks and involve you much of the time in the interview process as much or as little as you want. Even when hiring a team from a remote location like India or the Philippines, they can often provide teams who will also work in your time zone or even across multiple time zones. The ability to have backup team members who can test or do code reviews or provide documentation for a new feature during the off hours can increase productivity and speed up time to release considerably. The main concern is making sure they all feel part of the team again, as well as accountable for each other.

Hiring an agency can be very different than hiring a few consultants from your network or from Upwork or Fiverr. With an agency, you get oversight and management from within to help keep your team on track; you also get additional coworkers who can help team members from other projects in the agency. The more projects that the agency works on that are similar to us in technical requirements, the better the peer group for them to bounce technical ideas off.

The main drawbacks to the agency model though should be considered as well. Oftentimes you will have another internal team culture and process to work around, and while often they will adapt to your process and culture you need to make sure that is something the agency can facilitate. You also have to consider the fact that they may be working in a hybrid on-premises office with others and those ideas may be shared. That is a double-edged sword when it comes to technical problems. You get help from others who have done the work before, but you may be helping your competitors in certain technical areas gain ground. Oftentimes that's a risk worth taking because most technical challenges are solved quickly with online help and community sources anyway and a good engineering team won't be slowed down by these.

Adapting Processes for Remote Teams

Remote team members should be included in all team processes and activities, including sprint planning, check-ins, and even team and individual celebrations and all staff meetings. Use project management tools like Asana, Trello, or Jira to assign tasks and track progress, and use videoconferencing for remote team members to attend meetings and participate in team discussions. Ensure that all team members have access to the same information and that communication channels are clear and easily accessible. In this section, we'll delve deeper into adapting various team processes for remote teams.

Embrace Remote-Friendly Project Management Tools: Project management tools play a crucial role in keeping remote teams organized and productive. As mentioned earlier, platforms like Asana, Trello, or Jira allow teams to assign tasks, set deadlines, and track progress in real time. These tools also facilitate seamless collaboration as team members can comment on tasks, share files, and receive notifications. When implementing these tools, ensure that all team members are trained to use them effectively and that they have access to the necessary resources.

Encourage Virtual Team Meetings: Regular team meetings are crucial for keeping everyone informed, debating advancement, and resolving issues. These sessions are even more important for teams that work remotely. Conduct virtual meetings that promote face-to-face interactions using videoconferencing tools like Zoom, Microsoft Teams, or Google Meet (Figure 3-5). Better nonverbal signs and communication are made possible through video calls, which strengthens team relationships.

ZOOM MEETING

Figure 3-5. Zoom meeting

Active participation is crucial for all team members, especially those doing remote work, during meetings. Give remote team members plenty of chances to contribute to discussions, ask questions, and offer their ideas. To ensure that everyone on the team can attend without excessive difficulty, think about rearranging meeting times to accommodate different time zones. Plan to have your all staff and team meetings recorded and transcribed so that team members can watch later and contribute comments.

Encourage Transparency and Accountability: It's crucial to uphold transparency in remote teams when discussing project status, deadlines, and individual contributions. Access to pertinent project files, shared folders, and progress reports should be available to team members. This openness promotes trust and gives distant team members a sense of belonging to the group. Again make sure you have a system for comments in place so that all staff can contribute and leave comments open for at least 24 hours to accommodate time zones. Promote an environment of accountability where team members accept responsibility for their work and speak up when there are problems.

Celebrating Milestones and Achievements

Recognizing the accomplishments of remote team members is important for building team morale and keeping everyone engaged. Celebrate milestones and achievements by using tools like Slack, Microsoft Teams, or Skype to send a virtual high five, have a virtual happy hour, or even send a small gift to the team member's home address. Recognize the contributions of all team members, regardless of their location.

Create special threads or channels for team members to celebrate their accomplishments or thank their teammates for their work. This open acknowledgment allows everyone in the team to see and appreciate each other's contributions, boosting team morale and camaraderie.

Encourage team members to send GIFs, emojis, or virtual high fives to show their gratitude and congrats. These small actions go a long way in helping remote team members feel valued and included in the team's accomplishments.

Plan team meetings or virtual happy hours to foster a more social and relaxed atmosphere. These activities can be performed as a regular team-building exercise, after the end of a project or after the achievement of an important milestone. See Figure 3-6.

Figure 3-6. *"Watercooler" is a channel where team members can engage in nonwork-related discussions*

Team members might converse informally, play computer games, or exchange humorous stories at these events. Plan online team lunches or coffee breaks so that remote team members can connect with their internal colleagues via videoconferencing. Encourage the team to take a break from work so they may talk about things other than work and get to know one another better. Even across geographical barriers, this unstructured bonding time improves relationships and team dynamics.

Successful remote teams thrive on a culture of recognition and appreciation. By celebrating the contributions of all team members, regardless of their location, you cultivate a strong team spirit that fuels motivation and enhances collaboration. Celebrate not only the big wins but also the small victories as they collectively contribute to the overall success of your remote dream team.

Ensuring Clear Communication

Clear communication is critical for remote teams. Ensure that communication channels are clearly defined and that everyone knows how and when to communicate, as shown in Figure 3-7. Use email, chat, videoconferencing, or phone calls to keep in touch and encourage team members to communicate frequently. Consider setting up a weekly or biweekly check-in for remote team members to share updates and ask questions. Use services for instant messaging, such as Slack or Microsoft Teams, to enable brief, informal chats among team members. These systems promote a more dynamic and participatory work environment by enabling remote team members to communicate with coworkers without using the formality of an email.

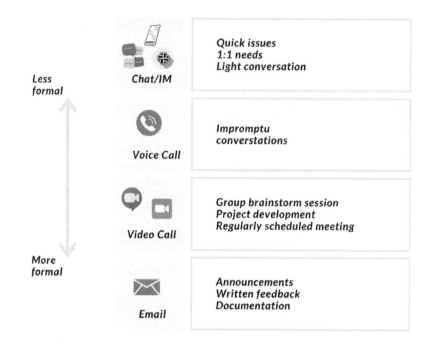

Figure 3-7. *Communication channels*

Make unique communication channels for particular projects or themes. This guarantees that conversations stay structured and that information is accessible to all parties. Check in on these channels frequently to quickly respond to queries or concerns.

Communication expectations should be established from the beginning. Create a communication policy that outlines response times, preferred communication channels, and acceptable working hours for remote team members. While some flexibility is essential, having clear expectations helps maintain accountability and ensures that everyone is on the same page.

Encourage a knowledge-sharing culture within the team. Remote team members might not have the same access to in-person knowledge exchanges, so make sure that information is readily available and shared transparently. Consider creating a centralized knowledge base, using shared documents or a company intranet, where team members can access essential resources, project updates, and best practices.

In global remote teams, time zone differences can be a significant challenge. When scheduling meetings or sending messages, be mindful of the varying time zones and try to find a balance that accommodates everyone's availability. Utilize scheduling tools that display multiple time zones to ease coordination.

Maintaining a Strong Team Culture

More than 50% of CEOs and CFOs say corporate culture influences productivity, creativity, profitability, firm value and growth rates. (Forbes)

Figure 3-8. *Forbes quote*

Remote team members should feel like they are part of the team, even if they are not physically present in the office. Encourage team bonding activities like virtual coffee breaks, book clubs, or even online gaming tournaments. Ensure that remote team members have access to the same resources as those in the office, such as training opportunities or company events.

Encourage a culture of inclusivity that values and appreciates the diverse perspectives and contributions of all team members, regardless of their location. Emphasize that every team member's input is valuable and that their voices will be heard and respected. Foster a collaborative environment where ideas can be freely shared and discussed.

Recognizing team members' birthdays and other special occasions demonstrates that you care about your remote team members as individuals, see Figure 3-8. Send virtual birthday cards or small gifts to celebrate these milestones, just as you would with in-house team members. Remembering and acknowledging personal events fosters a sense of belonging and shows that you value the human aspect of your remote dream team.

In an office setting, casual communication often happens naturally during breaks or at the watercooler. In remote teams, you can replicate this by creating dedicated channels for nonwork-related conversations. Encourage team members to discuss hobbies, interests, or current events in these channels. This informal chatter helps build rapport and creates a sense of community within the team.

Offer Equal Access to Opportunities: Ensure that remote team members have equal access to professional development opportunities, such as training sessions, workshops, or company events. If in-person events take place, consider offering virtual attendance options for remote team members to participate. Investing in their growth and development reinforces their value to the team and the organization.

In conclusion, managing remote teams requires a proactive approach to ensure that everyone is included and engaged. By hiring the right people, adapting processes, celebrating achievements, ensuring clear communication, and maintaining a strong team culture, remote teams can be just as effective as those working in the office. Remember that treating all team members equally, regardless of their location, is key to building a successful remote team.

Embracing Diversity in Remote Teams

Remote teams have the advantage of being able to hire from a global talent pool. This means that you can bring together people from different backgrounds, cultures, and skill sets. However, diversity in a remote team goes beyond just geography. It also includes cultural and gender diversity, as well as diversity in seniority level. Embracing diversity is crucial for creating a successful and efficient team (Figure 3-9).

Radical transparency acts as the cornerstone for successful remote teams operating within a diverse context. By adopting this approach, organizations ensure that all team members, regardless of location or background, have access to the same information and insights.

Figure 3-9. *Embracing diversity*

Diversity is an essential ingredient in innovation, creativity, and efficiency. Different backgrounds and experiences bring unique perspectives to problem-solving and idea generation. By bringing people with different ideas and opinions together, you can foster a culture of innovation and creativity. With the right mix of skills and personalities, teams can accomplish more than what any individual could do alone, and challenges of different opinions and ideas can drive innovation on a team and even help find problems before they become reality.

To promote diversity, it is essential to create an inclusive environment where everyone's opinions and ideas are respected and valued. Teams must embrace diversity in their hiring practices and ensure that people from all backgrounds have an equal opportunity to apply for and be hired for roles. This means actively seeking out diverse candidates and creating an inclusive hiring process. You shouldn't force diversity into your hiring decisions; instead, ensure that you are recruiting and hiring the best candidates by emphasizing the need for diversity on your teams to your hiring managers as well as in your recruitment and advertising efforts.

It is also important to provide diversity training for all team members to help them understand the importance of diversity and how to work effectively with people from different backgrounds. This training should cover topics such as cultural sensitivity, bias, and communication. Don't talk down to your coworkers; instead, focus on beneficial use cases they might not have seen while still covering the basics. Many will have been through similar diversity training and experiences already, so try to find new techniques and exercises while still getting the points across to those who might be new to the ideas.

In addition to diversity training, teams should also consider using collaboration tools that promote inclusivity, such as virtual whiteboards and brainstorming tools. These tools allow team members to work together in real time and contribute ideas without fear of judgment or discrimination.

To ensure that everyone has a voice, it's crucial to encourage open communication within the team. This means providing regular opportunities for team members to share their thoughts and ideas, whether through regular check-ins or team meetings. Team members should be encouraged to ask questions and provide feedback, regardless of their seniority level.

Celebrating diversity and team milestones is also important. This can be achieved by recognizing and rewarding team members for their contributions and achievements, whether through public acknowledgments, bonuses, or team outings. Celebrating team achievements can help to create a sense of community and motivate team members to continue to work together toward shared goals.

Harnessing Diversity and Remote Work for Enhanced Organizational Culture and Productivity

The modern business landscape is rapidly evolving, and organizations are recognizing the significant benefits of embracing diversity and remote work. This synthesis of diversity and remote work has the potential to revolutionize organizational culture, boost morale, and drive productivity. By fostering a work environment that embraces different perspectives, backgrounds, and talents and by leveraging the power of remote teams through radical transparency, organizations can create a dynamic ecosystem that thrives on innovation, collaboration, and success.

Diversity as a Catalyst for Positive Culture

Studies have consistently shown that diverse teams yield a myriad of benefits, ranging from improved problem-solving capabilities to enhanced creativity. According to a report by McKinsey & Company, companies with diverse executive boards tend to outperform their peers financially. When diversity becomes a fundamental part of an organization's DNA, it promotes a culture of inclusivity and mutual respect. Different viewpoints challenge conventional thinking and encourage a constant reevaluation of processes and practices, resulting in a culture that values innovation and progress. By recognizing and celebrating the unique strengths and perspectives of team members from various backgrounds, organizations create an environment where collaboration flourishes and morale receives a substantial boost.

Remote Work as a Catalyst for Enhanced Productivity

Remote work has become a pivotal component of modern work arrangements, offering benefits that extend beyond traditional office settings. According to research published by Stanford University, remote workers experience increased productivity due to fewer distractions and the flexibility to design their work environment. With remote work, teams can access global talent pools, bringing together professionals with diverse skills and expertise. However, the success of remote work hinges on transparent communication and collaboration. This is where radical transparency plays a vital role.

Radical Transparency: The Glue for Remote Diversity

Radical transparency acts as the cornerstone for successful remote teams operating within a diverse context. By adopting this approach, organizations ensure that all team members, regardless of location or background, have access to the same information and insights. This equal distribution of knowledge fosters a sense of inclusion and trust. For instance, a study in the *Harvard Business Review* suggests that teams operating remotely under conditions of radical transparency experience increased cooperation, as team members feel a greater sense of responsibility to contribute effectively. Furthermore, the clarity provided by radical transparency eliminates potential misunderstandings caused by geographical or cultural differences, enhancing collaboration and promoting a shared mission.

Cultivating Positive Culture and Enhanced Productivity

Organizations that embrace both diversity and remote work are positioned to harness a powerful synergy. By championing diversity in a remote context through radical transparency, organizations can create a culture that thrives on innovative thinking, open communication, and mutual respect. This approach aligns with the core principles of building a transparent culture in virtual work environments.

Organizations that combine diversity with remote work create a synergy where the unique strengths of diverse teams are amplified by the flexibility and inclusivity of remote work. This synergy leads to enhanced problem-solving, innovation, and creativity. When employees from various backgrounds collaborate remotely, they bring a broader spectrum of ideas and approaches to the table. Different perspectives encourage out-of-the-box thinking and the development of creative solutions. This dynamic mix of skills and viewpoints often leads to more comprehensive and innovative solutions to the challenges the organization faces.

Radical transparency plays a critical role in promoting employee engagement in a remote work environment. When an organization openly shares its achievements and challenges with remote employees, it creates a sense of belonging and investment among the remote workforce. These employees recognize that they are not merely isolated contributors but essential parts of the organization's journey. This transparency helps remote workers align their efforts with the company's goals and values, leading to a greater commitment to the organization's success.

Sources:

1. McKinsey & Company. (2018). Delivering Through Diversity. Retrieved from `www.mckinsey.com/ capabilities/people-and-organizational- performance/our-insights/delivering-through- diversity`

2. Stanford University. (2020). The Productivity Pitfalls of Working From Home in the Age of COVID-19. Retrieved from https://news.stanford. edu/2020/03/30/productivity-pitfalls-working-home-age-covid-19/

3. *Harvard Business Review*. (2022). Why Startups Should Embrace radical transparency Retrieved from https://hbr.org/2022/11/why-startups-should-embrace-radical-transparency

Review

Therapist 1: "Well, it's quite evident that remote work is the future, my friend. The data from Stanford University doesn't lie – remote workers are more productive, and they have the luxury of crafting their own workspaces. It's like having your own office, and you can even work in your pajamas."

Therapist 2: "Ah, the joys of remote work, indeed. But you see, it's not just about working in your pajamas. It's about embracing the diversity that remote work brings. We're not limited by geography anymore. We can hire the best talent from around the globe and create a diverse dream team."

Therapist 1: "True, true. Diversity is essential, and remote work opens up a world of possibilities. But you know what keeps all these remote teams together and functioning smoothly? Radical transparency. It's the glue that ensures everyone, no matter where they are, has the same information and can work in harmony."

Therapist 2: "Harmony is crucial, my friend, but it's not just about data. It's about culture. Remote teams need a positive culture to thrive. When you blend diversity with radical transparency, you get a culture that's like a symphony – innovative, communicative, and respectful."

Therapist 1: "A symphony of culture, indeed. But let's not forget the productivity boost. Radical transparency in diverse remote teams leads to

increased cooperation. People feel responsible for their contributions, and the clarity prevents misunderstandings caused by differences in location and culture."

Therapist 2: "Ah, cooperation and responsibility, the sweet sounds of a well-orchestrated team. But it goes even further. A diverse remote team with radical transparency experiences higher job satisfaction, trust in management, and problem-solving abilities. It's like music to the ears of any organization."

Therapist 1: "Music to the ears, indeed. So, my friend, it's clear that remote work, diversity, and radical transparency are a powerful trio. They shape organizational culture, boost productivity, and drive success in our ever-changing world."

Therapist 2: "Absolutely, my colleague. It's a trio that can't be beaten. Here's to the future of work – remote, diverse, and harmonious."

Therapist 1: "Cheers to that, my friend. Cheers to that."

CHAPTER 4

Therapy Is for the Clouds

Ok, so while we acknowledge that radical therapy and its philosophy for teams can certainly apply to all technical or even nontechnical work groups or teams, we're going to bring in some real-world examples now on how it can be used to revolutionize software development. We are going to talk specifically about cloud-native software development because let's face it, that is where most development is happening now along with AI and each will continue to grow together.

Along with this, we are going to talk about the preferred tools and processes we recommend and how they apply to almost any organization that creates products that use or implement software. Much of our focus will also be about open source tools and methods and how open source communities are built and maintained, so we will share those resources with you as well. Our goal is to create a community of transparency and open source enthusiasts with this book, but you don't have to be one or the other or even feel like you have to share if you don't want to.

Now, you may be asking yourself, what the heck is cloud-native development? Are we talking about coding while skydiving? Well no, we are really just talking about hosted services and virtual machines and the variety of ways we can access those services for software development as shown in Figure 4-1.

G. Lind and M. Mishchenko, *Radical Therapy for Software Development Teams,*
https://doi.org/10.1007/979-8-8688-0187-7_4

Also fair warning, we are going to get very technical, and that means jargon! We are going to include a glossary for these terms both inline in this book and a reference at the end of the book with links. If it gets too heavy or not interesting for you, then feel free to skip over those particular terms and case studies. We will have more at the end that take these approaches into other non-software contexts.

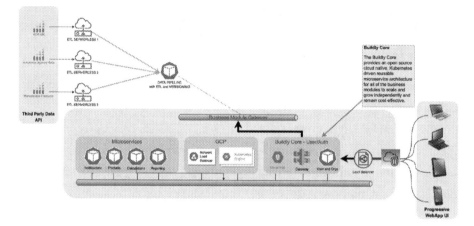

Figure 4-1. *Microservice cloud-native architecture*

So, how do we make cloud "native" development a reality and bring in radical transparency? First, we start with the architecture of cloud-native (Figure 4-1) and breaking up functionality into a set of centralized services in containers that are connected via APIs. Usually, this is called microservices, and we will stick with that for our purposes, but in reality, how you decide to set up your internal architecture is less important than how you set up and connect to those services. What is a microservice, you ask? Think of it like breaking down your software into tiny pieces of individual or grouped functionality like little clouds, each with their own job to do. This makes it easier to develop, test, and deploy your applications, all while increasing scalability and reliability.

But we can't stop there. We also need to embrace continuous integration and continuous delivery (CI/CD). This means that we're constantly testing and deploying new code so that we can catch and fix any issues as quickly as possible. And last but not least, we need to monitor our applications in the cloud. With the right monitoring tools, we can keep an eye on our applications and make sure they're running smoothly, all while gathering valuable data that can help us improve our software.

Now, you may be thinking, "Wow, that sounds like a lot of work." But fear not because the radical therapy philosophy combined with our preferred tools can make it fast, easy, and dare I say it, fun! So let's dive headfirst into the cloud and start building some amazing software.

Definition of Cloud-Native Software Development and Its Benefits for Modern Software Development

Cloud-native software development is a modern approach to software development that focuses on creating applications that are optimized for cloud environments. In simple terms, it's like building software that lives on one more hosting provider–specific clouds and is designed to scale and grow in that environment.

The benefits of cloud-native software development are many. First and foremost, it allows for rapid development and deployment of software applications. It also enables automatic scaling of resources as needed, which means your application can handle increased traffic without breaking a sweat. Additionally, it provides enhanced security, resilience, and reliability for your applications. Another important aspect is in the back-end architecture and how it allows developers to build applications in components and maintain and develop those components individually.

This idea allows the developers to work on code blocks that create specific sets of functionality without having to worry about version control systems creating conflicts. Conflicts in version control (see Figure 4-2) can create havoc on a developer's productivity, and allowing a developer to run his own blocks of code in a service on its own eliminates the "two many cooks in the kitchen" problem in version control systems like GitHub.

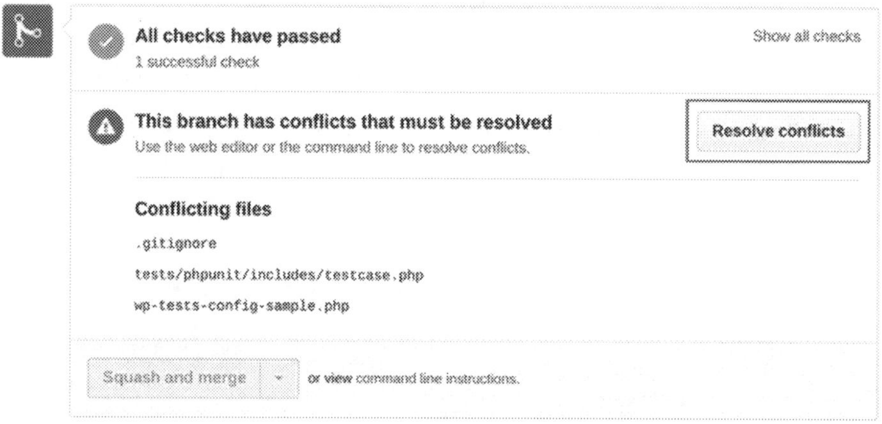

Figure 4-2. *Conflicts in version control*

Two key technologies that enable cloud-native software development are Kubernetes and Docker. Kubernetes is an open source container orchestration platform that automates the deployment, scaling, and management of containerized applications (Figure 4-3).

What is Kubernetes?

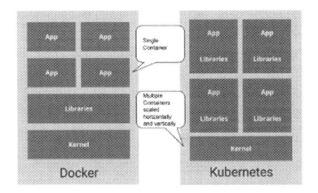

Figure 4-3. *Kubernetes*

Docker, on the other hand, is a containerization platform that allows developers to package an application and all its dependencies into a single container that can be easily moved between environments (Figure 4-4).

What is Docker?

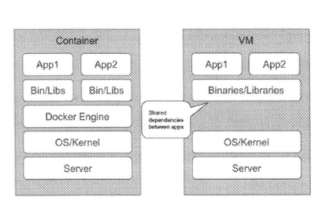

Figure 4-4. *Docker*

Another key benefit of cloud-native software development is the ability to deploy applications across multiple cloud providers. This is known as multicloud deployment, and it provides greater flexibility and redundancy for your applications. In the event of a failure in one cloud provider, your application can continue running on another provider without any interruption.

Cloud-native software development is all about building applications that are optimized for cloud environments. It provides rapid development and deployment, automatic scaling, enhanced security and reliability, and the ability to deploy across multiple cloud providers. By using tools like Kubernetes and Docker, developers can easily create cloud-native applications that can thrive in any environment.

Strategies for Cloud-Native Teams

When it comes to implementing cloud-native software development practices in your team's workflow, there are a few strategies to consider. One important aspect is the use of common design patterns for cloud-native architecture. The Loosely Coupled–Share Nothing Pattern, Chained Design Pattern, Aggregator Design Pattern, Proxy Design Pattern, and Async Design Pattern are all examples of patterns that can help create a more scalable and flexible architecture, compared to a shared or monolithic approach to data.

In addition to design patterns, using open source tools allows you sometimes to have the best of all worlds in your application. With the open source tool Buildly Core (Figure 4-5), an API gateway for managing microservices, we were able to create our own Buildly Flex pattern. This pattern allows for microsites, right-sized business-driven services, or even monoliths to be easily created while still enabling simplified front-end queries via the data mesh. With Buildly Flex, teams can isolate functionality into services and work on different sections without conflict while still reusing core components as needed.

Figure 4-5. *The open source tool Buildly Core, an API gateway for managing microservices*

Overall, implementing cloud-native software development practices can help teams create more scalable, flexible, and reliable applications. Teams can get more productivity and effectiveness out of their development work by taking a more modular approach and using the appropriate tools and techniques.

Loosely Coupled–Share Nothing Pattern

This pattern is based on the idea that each service should be self-contained and independent of other services. In this pattern, each service has its own data store, and communication between services is done through lightweight protocols like REST. This approach helps to reduce the risk of a single point of failure and makes it easier to scale individual services as needed.

Chained Design Pattern

In this pattern (Figure 4-6), each service depends on the output of another service, forming a chain of services. This approach helps to break down complex business logic into smaller, more manageable pieces. However, it can create dependencies that can be difficult to manage and can increase the risk of a cascading failure if one service in the chain fails.

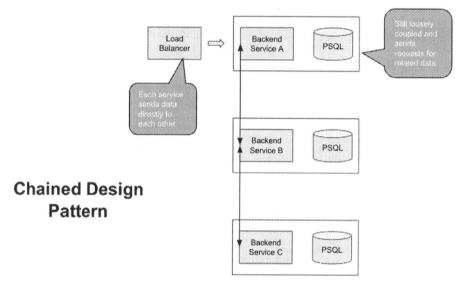

Figure 4-6. *Chained Design Pattern*

Aggregator Design Pattern

In this pattern (Figure 4-7), a single service is responsible for collecting data from multiple services and aggregating it into a single response. This approach can help to simplify the user experience by presenting a single view of multiple data sources. However, it can create a single point of failure if the aggregator service fails and can increase the risk of data inconsistencies if data is not synchronized properly between services.

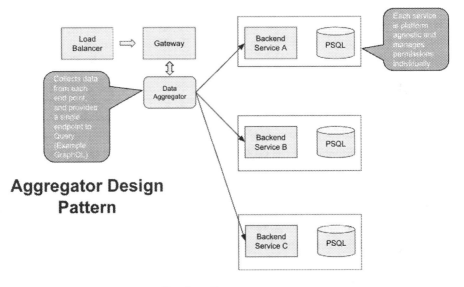

Figure 4-7. *Aggregator Design Pattern*

Proxy Design Pattern

In this pattern (Figure 4-8), a proxy service acts as an intermediary between the client and the server. The proxy service can cache responses, route requests to the appropriate service, and handle authentication and authorization. This approach can help to improve performance and reduce the load on individual services. However, it can create additional network latency and can increase the complexity of the overall system.

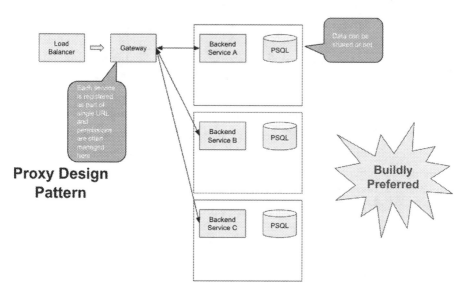

Figure 4-8. *Proxy Design Pattern*

Async Design Pattern

In this pattern (Figure 4-9), services communicate with each other asynchronously, using messaging systems like Apache Kafka or RabbitMQ. This approach helps to decouple services and reduce dependencies and can make it easier to handle large volumes of data. However, it can increase the complexity of the system and can require additional infrastructure to manage the messaging system.

Loosely Coupled - Shared Data - Patterns

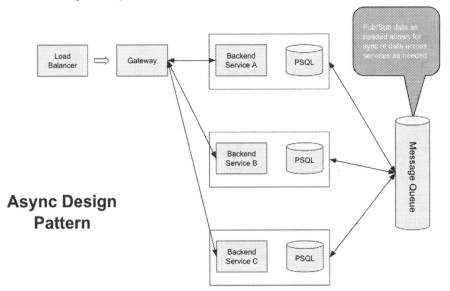

Async Design Pattern

Figure 4-9. *Async Design Pattern*

When it comes to working on code without conflict using microservices, the key is to design services that are as independent as possible. Each service should have a clearly defined scope and set of responsibilities and should communicate with other services only through well-defined APIs. This helps to reduce the risk of conflicts and makes it easier for different teams to work on different services without stepping on each other's toes.

For example, imagine a team working on a microservice that handles user authentication. Another team is working on a microservice that handles user profiles. By defining clear APIs for each service, the teams can work independently without worrying about conflicts. The authentication service can expose an API for validating user credentials, and the profile service can use that API to ensure that the user is authenticated before returning profile information. As long as the APIs are well-defined and stable, the teams can work independently without conflict.

Microapps vs. Monolithic Apps in the Cloud

When it comes to cloud-native software development, one key decision is whether to adopt microapps or stick with monolithic applications. The choice between these two approaches can significantly impact how your team develops, deploys, and manages software in the cloud.

Microapps

Unlike conventional microservices that may rely on external components for user interface presentation, microapps redefine this paradigm by encapsulating not just specific functionalities or services but also housing their entire front end within their self-contained architecture.

This distinctive attribute sets microapps apart – they function akin to microservices but carry an added dimension. By encompassing all the required elements to serve the application, including the user interface, within their own defined space or container, microapps exhibit a heightened level of self-reliance and autonomy (see Figure 4-10).

This encapsulation fosters a self-sufficiency that is paramount in modern software development paradigms. It enables these microapps to operate seamlessly, minimizing external dependencies and streamlining deployment and management processes. Their self-contained nature empowers development teams with the ability to work on these entities independently, facilitating rapid development cycles and more efficient debugging.

Furthermore, this encapsulated architecture aligns harmoniously with the principles of agility, scalability, and resilience in the cloud environment. When confronted with challenges or issues, a microapp can be addressed and managed without impacting the broader system, underscoring its resilience and adaptability.

Monolithic Design Pattern

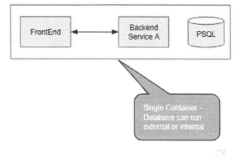

Mini App Design
Pattern

Figure 4-10. *Mini App Design Pattern*

Monolithic Apps

Monolithic applications (Figure 4-11), on the other hand, are like a grand, all-encompassing opera, where all the elements are tightly interwoven. In this approach, all the features and functions of an application are bundled into a single, cohesive unit. Monolithic apps have been around for a long time and have served their purpose well.

However, in the cloud-native era, they can sometimes be less suitable due to their size and complexity. Updating a monolithic app can be akin to renovating an entire opera house just to change one note in a song. This can slow down development cycles, hinder agility, and make it challenging to scale the application when needed. Additionally, monolithic apps can be less fault-tolerant, as a single issue can potentially disrupt the entire system.

Nonetheless, there are scenarios where monolithic apps make sense. For simple applications or situations where quick development and deployment aren't top priorities, monolithic apps can still be a reasonable choice. The cloud offers flexibility, and if the requirements align with a monolithic architecture, it can work effectively.

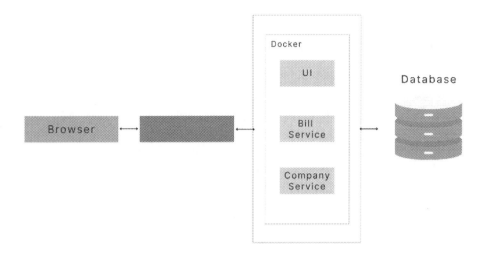

Figure 4-11. *Monolithic Apps Architecture*

Hybrid Approaches

It's worth noting that not all cloud-native applications fit neatly into one category. Some applications employ a hybrid approach, combining microapps and monolithic components. This can be particularly helpful for organizations transitioning from traditional on-premises applications to the cloud. By breaking down monolithic apps into smaller, more manageable microapps, organizations can gradually shift toward a more cloud-native architecture.

The choice between microapps, monolithic apps, and hybrid approaches in the cloud depends on the specific needs and goals of your organization. The cloud-native philosophy encourages flexibility and innovation, and the key is to select an architecture that aligns with your development speed, scalability requirements, and long-term vision. With the right strategy and tools, cloud-native software development can indeed revolutionize the way you create and manage software in the cloud, regardless of your chosen approach.

Review

Therapist 1: "Well, here we are, diving into the clouds – the digital ones, that is. Cloud-native development, my friend, it's the way of the future! No more coding while skydiving, though that would be quite the spectacle."

Therapist 2: "Indeed, my dear colleague, cloud-native development is where it's at. But let's be clear, we're not talking about coding on fluffy cumulus clouds. We're talking about creating software that lives on the digital cloud, with all the benefits that come with it."

Therapist 1: "Oh, absolutely. But fair warning, we're about to get technical, and that means jargon. So, if you start drowning in acronyms and terms, just skip over to the fun stuff. We'll have a glossary at the end for your rescue."

Therapist 2: "Ah, jargon, the language of the tech-savvy. But let's break it down for our friends here. Cloud-native development is about creating software that's optimized for the digital cloud. Think of it like building tiny digital clouds, each with its own job, making it easier to develop, test, and deploy."

Therapist 1: "Tiny digital clouds indeed! And we can't forget about continuous integration and continuous delivery – CI/CD for short. It's like a never-ending software party, always testing, always deploying. If there's a bug, we catch it before it causes trouble."

Therapist 2: "A never-ending party, you say? Well, who wouldn't want to be a part of that? And let's not forget about monitoring. No binoculars needed, my friend. With the right tools, we keep a watchful eye on our software and gather data to make it even better."

Therapist 1: "Watchful eyes and data-driven decisions, a match made in heaven. But, fear not, my friend, because with radical therapy philosophy and our beloved Buildly tools, all of this becomes a breeze. It's like turning a stormy cloud into a sunny day!"

Therapist 2: "A stormy cloud into a sunny day, indeed! So, here's to cloud-native development, where digital clouds reign supreme, and to a future of software that soars high above the tech landscape."

Therapist 1: "Cheers to that, my friend. Cheers to the clouds!"

CHAPTER 5

Cloud-Native Development within Radical Therapy Philosophy

Part of the broader radical therapy Development philosophy is the importance of cloud-native software development. This approach emphasizes the importance of building software that can be easily deployed and maintained in modern cloud environments. At the core of cloud-native software development is a focus on microservices, and while not every "cloud" application needs to be microservice driven, as we talked about before in most scenarios, breaking up the functionality of an app into truly independent functions, managed in their own repositories and with the ability to scale up or down independently from the rest of the application, can not only save you time but money as well.

Building a new software product or migrating away from a legacy system to the cloud can be daunting enough, but when you throw in the questions of architectures, cost, and estimation, many teams will get overwhelmed and look to proprietary solutions to get them going faster

© Gregory Lind, Maryna Mishchenko 2024
G. Lind and M. Mishchenko, *Radical Therapy for Software Development Teams*,
https://doi.org/10.1007/979-8-8688-0187-7_5

and hope that maintenance and support won't be a problem in the future. Here we'd like to discuss some options beyond proprietary solutions that offer increased flexibility as you move ahead.

Open Source

Hybrid proprietary and open source businesses and products are very common these days, maybe more so than you think. Even the biggest tech companies contribute and develop openly in open source repositories. Facebook, Google, Apple, and even Microsoft have vibrant open source communities built around many of their core business products and benefit tremendously from the community and code contributions. Even for us the radical therapists at Buildly have developed an open source core that can be used to facilitate cloud-native software development as we touched on previously. With the open source core, developers can create microservices and deploy them in containerized environments such as Kubernetes or Docker and then share those in an open source GitHub marketplace. This approach allows for faster iteration and deployment by removing redundancy around certain reusable services in applications while minimizing the risk of downtime or other issues when the traffic, data, and authentication are handled in the core. It was a no-brainer for us to build this open source, transparent from day one with GitHub commits every day in the initial development as well as feedback from internal and external developers.

Automating infrastructure management is a critical aspect of cloud-native software development. With open source tools, teams can automate the creation and management of infrastructure, including server instances, databases, and other services. This automation streamlines the process of creating and deploying services, reduces the risk of errors, and ensures that applications are always up-to-date. Using open source tools and building around those, contributing back to the originating communities and growing our own just makes sense. It increases our productivity and provides help in everything from bug fixes and detection, documentation, and design to new module development and sharing of innovations to speed up development, deployment, and more. It doesn't mean we have to do everything open source just because we have certain tools or processes that way, but we do try to build everything in an open source and transparent manner.

Open source projects and tools we use:

 Kubernetes: An open source container orchestration platform for automating the deployment, scaling, and management of containerized applications

 Docker: An open source platform for developing, shipping, and running applications in containers

 Prometheus: An open source monitoring and alerting toolkit designed for reliability and scalability

 Helm: A package manager for Kubernetes that simplifies deploying and managing applications in a Kubernetes cluster

 Istio: An open source service mesh that helps manage and secure microservices in a Kubernetes environment

 Knative: An open source platform to build, deploy, and manage serverless workloads on Kubernetes

 Envoy: An open source edge and service proxy designed for cloud-native applications

 Spinnaker: An open source continuous delivery platform designed for multicloud and microservices environments

Travis CI: A cloud-based continuous integration service that is often used for automating the build and deployment of cloud-native applications

Rancher: An open source container management platform that simplifies the management of Kubernetes clusters and containerized applications

Our primary tools are built around certain AI and machine learning technologies that are open source and help us to build a better product and release management solution, but the other components of that are proprietary and in private repositories. Managing deployments and releases can be challenging, so we built the Insights tools to help simplify this process, and we did it the same way we do manage our open source repositories. We include everyone from the business and development side in the product discussions and decision-making process, making sure we have leads that are encouraging feedback and then we use our own tools to make decisions, evaluate feedback, and plan releases.

Communication and Collaboration

Streamlining collaboration and issue tracking is a crucial aspect of cloud-native software development. Another thing we look for in tools is the ability to easily integrate with other tools, like GitHub and Trello, allowing teams to work together seamlessly without having to share logins or duplicate effort or documentation. With these tools well integrated via APIs or an API integration tool like Buildly Insights, developers can track issues, manage tasks, and collaborate on code changes, all within a single interface. It also facilitates better collaboration by creating multiple channels of communication that can be monitored by each user via their preferred method of communication. Allowing teams to monitor each other is an important part of transparency, but forcing new tools or new methods of communication creates a point of frustration. That's why it's important to use a tool like Insights that allows the connection of other preferred tools into one collective and collaborative environment, reducing tool and communication fatigue by adapting the notification processes of each team's preferred tool and process.

Development Team Management Tools We Use

Development Team Management:

 Buildly Insights: A product and release management platform that streamlines deployment and release planning, capacity optimization, and collaboration in software development.

Jira: A versatile project management tool by Atlassian that can be customized for agile software development, issue tracking, and team collaboration.

 Trello: A simple and visual project management tool, ideal for smaller teams and basic task management.

 Asana: A versatile work management tool that can help teams coordinate and manage their work.

 Basecamp: A user-friendly project management and team collaboration tool, known for its simplicity and communication features.

 Monday.com: A work operating system that empowers teams to run projects and workflows with confidence.

 Slack: A popular team communication and collaboration platform, which integrates with various project management tools and services.

Product Management:

 Buildly Insights: A product and release management platform that streamlines deployment and release planning, capacity optimization, and collaboration in software development.

Notion: A versatile all-in-one workspace for notes, tasks, wikis, and databases that can be used for product management documentation.

Confluence: A collaboration and documentation tool by Atlassian, often used for creating product requirement documents and technical documentation.

Miro: A collaborative online whiteboard platform for brainstorming, visualizing user journeys, and mapping out ideas.

Version Control and Collaboration:

 Git and GitHub: Git is a distributed version control system, and GitHub is a web-based platform that provides hosting for software development and collaboration.

 GitLab: A web-based DevOps platform that provides source code management (SCM), continuous integration, and more.

Slack: Slack platform is often used for real-time communication and collaboration within development teams.

Survey and Customer Support:

 SurveyMonkey: A popular survey platform that enables you to create and analyze surveys to gather valuable customer feedback.

 Zendesk: A customer support platform that provides help desk software, customer service, and engagement features.

 Google Forms: A simple and free tool for creating surveys and forms that can be easily shared and analyzed.

 Basecamp: Besides project management, Basecamp also offers collaboration tools to facilitate communication with customers and clients.

Videoconferencing:

 Google Meet: A videoconferencing tool by Google that provides secure and scalable online meetings

 Zoom: A popular videoconferencing platform that offers video meetings, webinars, and collaboration features

Software development that is cloud-native is a fundamental component of the radical therapy concept because it can help a business scale from 1 to a million customers without a need to re-architect and set up properly without a lot of additional overhead, but it's certainly not the only way to go and for software as well as for other types of technical and business collaborations radical therapy can help as well. Key to success though in any of those is finding a powerful tool that can integrate with others and that can be used to facilitate your approach. Let's look at some case studies of some similar types of products that use cloud-native as well as other architectural approaches.

Case Studies

Case Study 1: Ecommerce Site Release Management

We recently used the radical transparency process and cloud-native architectures to help an ecommerce company streamline their release management process. With a large team of developers working on a cloud-native architecture, keeping track of all the moving pieces was becoming a challenge. Adding to that problem was the fact that part of the team was remote and on contracts and the rest of the team worked in the corporate headquarters and worked in the office during regular business hours. Using radical transparency and a few new tools, the team was able to create a release plan that took into account business requirements, technical specifications, and capacity planning.

The team first set up integrations between Trello and GitHub. Business requirements were entered into Trello and linked to technical issues in GitHub where available. Each new feature or epic was then tagged and reviewed for accuracy from the business side and technical leads before GitHub tickets were created. We then proceeded to add "punch list" cards for each testing round to be followed up on so the backlog didn't get clogged with issues from testing vs. issues from production.

We then trained an LLM-based AI to give us suggestions to generate a release plan based on the technical documentation and capacity planning. The plan included estimated timelines, dependencies, and milestones. The team was able to easily adjust the plan as needed, with real-time updates visible to all team members. The team was included in reviewing the estimates from both sides but did not have to base their estimates on hunches or vague memories.

With a bit more transparency and few small automation steps, the team was able to significantly reduce the time and stress involved in release management. By automating the documentation process and providing clear timelines, team members could focus on development work rather than worrying about the release process.

Case Study 2: Healthcare Application Release Management

A healthcare software company was looking to improve their release management process for their monorepo application. They had a large team working on multiple features and releases simultaneously, with frequent changes and updates. They struggled with meeting deadlines because of the growth of the application, the lack of documentation from multitudes of previous in-house and outsourced developers, and the lack of transparency into the business decisions and changes that seemed to happen without any advanced notice. This team implemented a new transparency process as well as started to use Buildly Insights to manage release and create documentation. Business requirements were entered into Trello and linked to technical issues in GitHub using Buildly Insights then automatically transformed these issues into technical documentation, ensuring clear communication between stakeholders. They then implemented a lead review process where every new requirement or feature that came into the Trello backlog was co-reviewed by a business analyst and technical lead. This lynchpin team communicated to each side the need for more collaboration and transparency on each side of the request, received feedback when needed, and documented that into the process. At first, this slowed down development as the backlog was reviewed, but it also removed redundant or overlapping features reducing the overall backlog.

The team used Buildly Insights to create a release plan based on the technical documentation and capacity planning. The plan included milestones and dependencies, with AI-powered suggestions for improving timelines and avoiding conflicts. They were then able to automate the release status notifications so that the business side could easily track the progress of business critical features and the developers could focus on the backlog and testing without having to communicate status updates.

With Buildly Insights, the team was able to reduce the time and effort involved in release management while also improving communication and collaboration across teams. The platform's ability to translate business requirements into technical documentation and automate the release planning process helped the team stay on track and meet deadlines while also reducing stress and improving morale.

Cloud-Native Software Development Mastery: DevOps, Testing, and Team Collaboration for Success

1. Define your team's DevOps practices for deployment and testing. This means defining how your team will handle continuous integration, continuous delivery, and continuous deployment. For example, your team may decide to use a tool like Jenkins to automate builds and testing or use GitLab to create pipelines that automatically build and test code when changes are pushed to a repository.

2. Review use cases and requirements with the team. Before starting development, it's important to review the requirements and use cases with the team to ensure everyone is on the same page. This can involve using a tool like Buildly Insights to communicate the requirements and track progress.

3. Create test environments. Your team should have a separate environment for testing so that you can catch any issues before they make it to production. This can involve creating a staging environment that mirrors the production environment.

4. Create ephemeral testing environments. Ephemeral testing environments allow you to test specific changes without affecting the rest of the application. For example, you could spin up a temporary environment to test a new feature or bug fix.

5. Enable local development with daily check-ins. Allowing developers to work on their local machines can speed up development and make it easier for them to test their code. Daily check-ins ensure that everyone is aware of what's being worked on and can identify and resolve any conflicts early on.

6. Provide positive feedback during pull requests and reviews. Providing positive feedback during code reviews can help improve team morale and encourage collaboration. This can involve using a tool like Buildly Insights to track reviews and provide feedback to team members.

Using a product communication and planning tool can help facilitate these practices and make it easier for teams to work together. For example, Buildly Insights can be used to manage Jenkins builds and pipelines, track progress on requirements and use cases, and provide feedback during code reviews. By using a tool like Buildly Insights, teams can streamline their workflow and focus on delivering high-quality software.

Optimizing Cloud-Native Software Development: Strategies and Tools for Success

1. Start by adopting cloud-native architecture and design patterns, such as the Loosely Coupled, Share Nothing, Chained, Aggregator, Proxy, and Async patterns. Develop microservices that can be independently deployed and scaled. Use Kubernetes and Docker to containerize and manage these microservices.

2. Use a product communication and planning tool like Buildly Insights to set up a product road map and backlog of features and priorities that align with your organization's mission, vision, and goals. Set up a project board and use it to track business requirements, issues, and feature requests. Use labels and milestones to organize your tasks and track progress. Get everyone on the same page and use the same nomenclature, taxonomy, and labels wherever possible.

3. Automate infrastructure management with open source tools. Use Terraform templates to provision and manage your cloud infrastructure. Use a gateway like Buildly's Open Source Core and Kubernetes operator to deploy and manage your microservices on Kubernetes. Use a CI/CD pipeline to automate your build, test, and deployment process.

4. Wherever you can, try and use one tool to manage deployments and releases that everyone has access to. Find a good release planning feature or

template to plan and schedule your releases; the
features inside many product management tools
include road mapping but rarely include release
management as Buildly Insights does, but if nothing
else, look for a tool that can integrate with others via
API management and connections. Once you have
a good road map set up for your initial vision, start
planning releases as far out as you can and use AI
tools to guide you with suggestions and an estimate
of the required capacity needed to meet each
release deadline.

5. Streamline collaboration and issue tracking with
    GitHub and Trello integrations. Use GitHub to
    manage your code and issues. Use Trello to track
    your business requirements and feature requests.
    Use Buildly Insights to connect these two platforms
    and provide a unified view of your product
    development process.

6. Implement DevOps practices for deployment and
    testing. Use review and feedback processes, such
    as pull requests and code reviews, to ensure code
    quality and reduce errors. Use test environments,
    such as ephemeral testing environments and local
    development environments, to catch issues early
    in the development process. Use daily checking
    and positive feedback to promote a culture of
    continuous improvement and growth.

Review

Therapist 1: Today, we're diving into the world of cloud-native development, but it's not just tech – it's a whole philosophy!

Therapist 2: Ah, the cloud! It sounds so... ethereal.

Therapist 1: (laughs) Well, it's a bit more grounded than that. It's about building software that's scalable, resilient, and always available.

Therapist 2: So, it's like giving your software a superpower?

Therapist 1: You could say that! And this chapter talks about tools and processes that help teams do just that.

Therapist 2: Oh realllly? Tell me more.

Therapist 1: Many product and project management tools help create documentation while assigning issues and tasks to the technical team members and can even schedule meetings and set up calls. All the nitty-gritty stuff.

Therapist 2: Ah, so it's like a personal assistant for developers.

Therapist 1: Absolutely! And it's all about radical transparency and streamlining collaboration.

Therapist 2: Radical transparency? That sounds intense!

Therapist 1: Well, it's about being open and honest, sharing what you're working on, and making sure everyone's on the same page. And to be honest, the authors work with Buildly, so you can understand why they would recommend it, but they also offer other ways and other tools that do similar things.

Therapist 2: Like group therapy for teams!

Therapist 1: (laughs) Yes, in a way! And this chapter even has some case studies. One's about an ecommerce company that used transparency to simplify their release management.

Therapist 2: So, it's like a success story from therapy?

Therapist 1: Exactly! It helped them communicate better and reduce stress in their team.

Therapist 2: That's the kind of therapy I like to hear about!

Therapist 1: You've got it! It's all about making product development a more pleasant and efficient experience.

Therapist 2: Well, sign me up for some more radical therapy!

Therapist 1: (laughs) It's a therapy session everyone should consider.

CHAPTER 6

Radical Process

Here we will give you two examples of Radical Process, the first for software development and the second for technical development of a similar nature that is not software.

For software, Radical Process is an adaptable and flexible approach to software development that puts collaboration, communication, and continuous improvement at the forefront. Based on agile principles, Radical Process streamlines the development process with a lightweight planning structure and focuses on the first step of the process to ensure that the project has a strong foundation from the start.

First Steps

Step 1: Define Your Project's Vision (Timeline: 1 week)

- Start by clearly defining the vision and goals of your software project. What problem does it aim to solve? What is the intended impact?

Step 2: Assemble a Truly Diverse Team (Timeline: 2 weeks)

- Form a cross-functional team that includes developers, designers, product managers, and stakeholders. Ensure diversity in terms of skills, experiences, and perspectives.

© Gregory Lind, Maryna Mishchenko 2024
G. Lind and M. Mishchenko, *Radical Therapy for Software Development Teams,*
https://doi.org/10.1007/979-8-8688-0187-7_6

Step 3: Kickoff Meeting (Timeline: 2 days)

– Hold a kickoff meeting to introduce the project to the team. Discuss the project's goals, vision, and the importance of radical transparency in the process.

Step 4: Choose Collaboration Tools (Timeline: 1 week)

– Select collaboration tools that facilitate transparency, such as project management software, version control systems, and communication platforms. Ensure that everyone has access and understands how to use them.

Step 5: Create a Detailed Project Road Map (Timeline: 2 weeks)

– Work collaboratively to create a detailed project road map. This should include milestones, features, and estimated timelines.

Step 6: Develop a Transparent Documentation Strategy (Timeline: 1 week)

– Establish a documentation strategy that covers everything from project requirements to technical specifications. Use a version-controlled documentation system.

Step 7: Embrace Open Communication (Timeline: Ongoing)

– Encourage open and honest communication within the team. Use regular stand-up meetings, video calls, and chat channels to facilitate discussions.

Step 8: Share Progress Publicly (Timeline: Every 2 weeks)

– Share progress updates and milestones with stakeholders and the broader community. Use blogs, newsletters, or social media to keep everyone informed.

Step 9: Gather Feedback Continuously (Timeline: Ongoing)

– Actively seek feedback from team members, stakeholders, and end users. Make it easy for people to provide input, and be receptive to suggestions.

Step 10: Adapt and Iterate (Timeline: Every 2 weeks)

– Embrace a culture of adaptation and iteration. Use feedback to refine your project continually. Be willing to pivot if necessary.

Step 11: Celebrate Successes (Timeline: Ongoing)

– Recognize and celebrate achievements and milestones, both big and small. This boosts morale and reinforces the value of transparency.

Step 12: Resolve Conflicts Transparently (Timeline: As needed)

– If conflicts arise within the team, address them openly and transparently. Encourage a culture of respectful disagreement and problem-solving.

Step 13: Document and Share Failures (Timeline: As needed)

– Don't hide failures or setbacks. Document them transparently and share the lessons learned. Failure can be a valuable source of knowledge.

Step 14: Stay Committed to Transparency (Timeline: Ongoing)

– Radical transparency is an ongoing commitment. Ensure that it remains a core principle throughout the project's life cycle.

Step 15: Evaluate and Improve (Timeline: Every 3 months)

– Periodically evaluate the effectiveness of your transparency practices. Solicit feedback on how to improve the process further.

In Radical Process, the first steps are process and documentation driven and can be adjusted and reduced in your future projects once you have an organization bought into the process and transparency. Once you start iterating in step 10 (adapt and iterate), your first iterations should be focused or centered on UI design, integrated with data models and business requirements. This approach allows for a high-level understanding of the project goals and requirements and creates epics or high-level features based on business language that is handed off to the developers for feedback and translation to technical specifications and estimates. This ensures that the development team has a clear understanding of the business requirements and can provide accurate estimates for the project timeline.

At every step of the process, each team member has a light touch oversight, ensuring that the project stays on track and meets the goals of the business. With Radical Process, the focus is on communication and collaboration, making sure that each member of the team is empowered to contribute their ideas and expertise. The result is a streamlined, efficient development process that delivers high-quality software that meets the needs of the business.

Example

Epic: Social Media Integration
    User Stories:

1. As a user, I want to be able to sign in to the app using my Facebook or Twitter account.

2. As a user, I want to be able to share content from the app on my Facebook or Twitter account.

3. As a user, I want to be able to see content from my Facebook or Twitter feed within the app.

Breakdown into GitHub Issues:

Microservice 1 – Authentication Service:

1. Create an OAuth2 client for Facebook and Twitter login.

2. Add API endpoints for Facebook and Twitter login.

3. Store OAuth2 tokens in the database for future use.

4. Add logic to check if the user is already registered before creating a new account.

5. Add logic to handle Facebook and Twitter API responses.

6. Store shared content metadata in the database.

Front-End UI Repository:

Microservice 2 – Social Media Service:

1. Create API endpoints to share content on Facebook and Twitter.

2. Add logic to handle Facebook and Twitter API responses.

3. Store shared content metadata in the database.

Front-End UI Repository:

1. Add Facebook and Twitter login buttons to the login page.

2. Add Facebook and Twitter share buttons to content pages.

3. Create a feed component to display Facebook and Twitter content in the app.

Issue Backlogs:

Microservice 1 – Authentication Service:

1. Create an OAuth2 client for Facebook and Twitter login.

2. Add API endpoints for Facebook and Twitter login.

3. Store OAuth2 tokens in the database for future use.

4. Add logic to check if the user is already registered before creating a new account.

Microservice 2 – Social Media Service:

1. Create API endpoints to share content on Facebook and Twitter.

2. Add logic to handle Facebook and Twitter API responses.

3. Store shared content metadata in the database.

Front-End UI Repository:

1. Add Facebook and Twitter login buttons to the login page.

2. Add Facebook and Twitter share buttons to content pages.

3. Create a feed component to display Facebook and Twitter content in the app.

This is the start of a flexible framework for software development teams that emphasizes lightweight planning and a loaded first step that focuses on UI design integrated with data models and business requirements. Daily transparency check-ins are a crucial aspect of the Radical Process that can benefit software development teams in several ways, but what we are really doing is sharing everything openly from the start and asking for feedback where we can. Rather than planning every detail, or spending hours in backlog grooming sessions, we are using the communication tools we have to collaborate and build requirements together and ask for help where needed.

Firstly, transparency check-ins foster a culture of accountability and promote trust among team members. By providing daily updates on progress, challenges, and roadblocks, team members are able to work collaboratively and address issues in a timely manner. This not only reduces the risk of delays or errors but also builds a sense of camaraderie and shared responsibility within the team.

Secondly, they allow for more effective project management by providing up-to-date information on project status and enabling teams to identify potential issues early on. This allows for quick adjustments to be made to timelines, resources, and priorities, reducing the risk of project failure and ensuring that stakeholders are kept informed throughout the development process.

To implement the Radical Process and daily transparency check-ins in your team's workflow, consider the following strategies:

1. Define your team's goals and priorities (Figure 6-1), and develop a shared understanding of what success looks like for each project. Create a project vision statement and list of key objectives and share that openly in a GitHub repo ReadME file.

⊟ README.md

Buildly-Core Project Goals and Vision

Project Vision

Buildly-Core is designed to be a cornerstone component for cloud-native architectures, providing a versatile gateway and service discovery system for microservices. Our vision is to simplify the integration of data services, APIs, and endpoints, offering a lightweight and easy-to-use solution that connects them all through a single, accessible URL.

Key Objectives

- Simplified Integration: Streamline the integration of diverse data services, APIs, and endpoints into a unified gateway, making it easier for developers to work with microservices.
- Lightweight and High Performance: Prioritize performance optimization to ensure that Buildly-Core remains lightweight and responsive even in high-traffic environments.
- Service Discovery: Implement robust service discovery mechanisms to enable dynamic service registration and discovery for microservices within the architecture.
- Security and Access Control: Implement security measures to protect against unauthorized access and ensure data and services are secure.
- Flexibility and Scalability: Design Buildly-Core to be flexible and scalable, accommodating future growth and evolving architectural needs.
- Documentation and Ease of Use: Provide comprehensive documentation and resources to make it easy for developers to understand and work with Buildly-Core.
- Community Support: Foster a supportive community where developers can collaborate, seek help, and share insights and best practices.

Figure 6-1. *Buildly-Core Project Goals and Vision*

2. Break down project features or epics into smaller user stories and create GitHub issues or tasks for each microservice and front-end repository.

3. Hold daily stand-ups via a remote tool like Slack to provide updates on progress and identify any issues or roadblocks. Make sure to encourage transparency and accountability among team members.

4. Follow up your remote stand-ups with end-of-day handoffs that relay what you have finished, what is left, and what you need help with in the same tool.

5. Make sure that each new process you add is repeatable and has a flexible framework that can be easily adapted to new projects and changing circumstances. This can help reduce confusion and ensure that all team members are on the same page. If you are a large organization with multiple projects and team members moving back and forth, you need processes and frameworks that are similar to reduce onboarding time.

Software development teams may improve stakeholder outcomes, manage projects more efficiently, and collaborate more effectively by putting the Radical Process and daily transparency check-ins into practice.

Check-Ins and Transparency

Daily code check-ins on GitHub can greatly enhance transparency and accountability within a development team. By regularly pushing small, incremental changes to the code base, team members can better track the progress of their work and collaborate more effectively. This approach helps to reduce the size and complexity of each individual change, making it easier for other team members to review and provide feedback. It also helps to prevent duplication of effort and reduce the risk of conflicts arising between different parts of the code base.

Incorporating daily check-ins into daily stand-ups helps to ensure that everyone is aware of what has been accomplished since the previous check-in and what is planned for the next 24 hours. During stand-ups, team members can review the check-in hashes to identify any potential issues or conflicts that need to be addressed. This also allows for easier tracking of changes and can help identify any areas of the code base that may require further attention or optimization.

Peer reviews of check-ins and pull requests can further enhance the quality of code and ensure that everyone is adhering to best practices and coding standards. By requiring team members to review each other's work before it is merged into the main code base, it helps to catch potential bugs or errors early on in the development process. Additionally, this approach promotes a culture of collaboration and knowledge sharing, where team members can learn from one another and develop new skills.

Overall, daily check-ins and peer reviews are an essential part of the Radical Process, promoting transparency, accountability, and collaboration within the development team. Through the implementation of these principles in daily stand-ups and other development process parts, teams may guarantee that all members are working toward a single objective and producing excellent software in a timely and effective manner.

Example Code

Checkin:Fixes #123: Updated authentication flow to fix user login issue.

In this fix, the authentication flow was updated to properly handle user logins, including handling of invalid credentials and token expiration. Also, update the user model to include additional fields for better tracking of user activity.

Example Stand-Up

Yesterday, I fixed the user login issue by updating the authentication flow and user model. The code check-in for this can be found here: [link].

Today, I will be working on the user profile page, and I am currently blocked by the need to confirm the design with the UX team. I will reach out to them today to discuss and hopefully get unblocked.

Case Study 1

Company X is a midsized software development firm that has been experiencing difficulties in delivering projects on time and within budget. The company decided to implement the Radical Process, which is a flexible and adaptive framework that emphasizes collaboration and transparency.

The company started by creating user stories in Trello, which were used to develop a set of high-level features or epics. The epics were then broken down into smaller pieces of work in GitHub, with each microservice and front-end repository having its own set of issues.

The development team was able to communicate better and collaborate more effectively using this process. By working together to define the requirements and breaking down the work into smaller, manageable pieces, the team was able to gain a better understanding of the project and what needed to be done.

Daily check-ins were implemented to ensure that everyone was aware of what was being worked on and any issues that had arisen. This helped to reduce the risk of miscommunication and misunderstanding.

The team also implemented peer code reviews and daily code check-ins on GitHub. This allowed for more frequent feedback and ensured that code was being reviewed and tested regularly. By checking in code daily, the team was able to catch errors and address them quickly, without letting them build up.

The Radical Process also helped to establish clear timelines for the project. By breaking down the work into smaller pieces and working iteratively, the team was able to identify and address any issues early on in the development process. This helped to reduce the risk of delays and ensure that the project was delivered on time.

Overall, implementing the Radical Process had a significant impact on the success of the project. By promoting collaboration and transparency, the team was able to work together more effectively and deliver a high-quality product on time and within budget.

Best Practices

Sure, here are some best practices for maintaining transparency and accountability in software development teams using the radical therapy approach and the tools mentioned in the Radical Process:

- Use a communication and planning tool like Buildly Insights or Trello to document user stories, features, and epics and ensure that everyone on the team can access and update them as needed. This creates a shared understanding of what needs to be built and why and allows everyone to contribute to the planning process.

- Break down features and epics into smaller, more manageable pieces that can be assigned to individual developers or teams. This makes it easier to track progress and ensure that everyone is working toward the same goals.

- Use a version control system like Git and require developers to commit their code changes frequently. This allows for easy tracking of changes and makes it easier to identify issues and resolve conflicts.

- Conduct daily stand-up meetings where each team member shares what they worked on the previous day, what they plan to work on that day, and any blockers they're facing. This keeps everyone on the same page and helps identify issues early on.

- Use a code review process where other developers review each other's code changes and provide feedback. This helps ensure code quality and consistency and allows for knowledge sharing among team members.

- Use automated testing tools to ensure that code changes don't introduce new bugs or issues. This helps catch issues early and saves time in the long run.

- Use performance metrics and analytics tools to measure progress and identify areas for improvement. This provides objective data to help guide decision-making and improve team performance.

By following these guidelines, teams may keep their software development processes transparent and accountable. This can promote better teamwork, streamline processes, and eventually produce software that is of higher quality.

Radical Process for Non-Software Products

In this adaptation for a non-software technical process, let's say you're revamping a manufacturing assembly line for a cutting-edge electric car. Here's how Radical Process could work:

Step 1: Blueprint Integration

Before anything else, focus on designing the user experience (in this case, the assembly line) in sync with data models and business requirements. Translate your manufacturing goals into "epics" or major features, just like software features but applied to car manufacturing. Hand these off to your engineers for feedback and technical specifications.

Ensure that your engineers and the production team have a clear understanding of what the assembly line should achieve. This ensures that everyone's on the same page and you get accurate estimates for the project timeline.

Step 2: Daily Transparency Check-Ins

Just like in software development, daily transparency check-ins are vital for accountability and teamwork. Every team member briefly shares what they accomplished, any challenges they encountered, and if there are any roadblocks. This daily ritual fosters trust, quick issue resolution, and a sense of shared responsibility within the manufacturing team.

Step 3: Continuous Improvement

Transparency check-ins also feed into continuous improvement. By resolving problems when they come up, you make on-the-fly adjustments to timelines, resources, and priorities. This reduces the risk of project failure and keeps stakeholders informed about the manufacturing process's progress.

Example

Imagine the epic here is "Implementing Advanced Robotics." It involves automating parts of the assembly process using cutting-edge robots. Here's how you'd break it down:

Engineering Team

- Develop a prototype robot arm capable of precise movements.

- Create an API for the robot arm's software to communicate with the assembly line.

- Establishasystemtomonitortherobot'sperformanceandmakereal-time adjustments.

- Address any safety concerns regarding robot–human interaction.

- Integrate the robot arm into the assembly line with minimal disruption.

Production Team

- Ensure the assembly line's layout accommodates the robot arm.

- Train assembly line workers to work alongside the robot safely.

- Develop procedures for maintenance and troubleshooting of the robot arm.

- Monitor production metrics to assess the robot arm's impact on efficiency and quality.

Daily Transparency Check-In

- Engineer: "Yesterday, we successfully integrated the robot arm's API with the assembly line software. Here's the code commit: [link]. Today, we'll focus on real-time monitoring."

- Production Manager: "Yesterday, we trained workers on robot safety protocols, and today, we'll monitor their interaction with the robot closely."

Case Study 2

Company XYZ, a manufacturing firm, was facing challenges in modernizing their production process. They adopted the Radical Process to streamline the transition. Breaking down their epic, "Automated Production," into manageable tasks allowed for better communication between engineers and production staff.

Daily transparency check-ins enabled swift issue resolution. For example, when engineers faced challenges in robot integration, they quickly reached out to the production team for insights, reducing delays. The process's transparency also enabled the identification of bottlenecks, optimizing workflows.

By adopting the Radical Process for non-software technical processes, Company XYZ delivered their automated production line on time and within budget. The culture of collaboration and accountability created by the process led to a successful outcome.

Best Practices

To maintain transparency and accountability in non-software technical processes using the Radical Process, consider these best practices:

1. Use a shared documentation tool, like a digital whiteboard or project management software, to record project details, goals, and progress. Keep it accessible to all team members.

2. Break down complex projects into smaller tasks and clearly assign responsibilities to individuals or teams.

3. Encourage daily check-ins, even for non-software processes. Share updates, challenges, and plans to keep everyone informed.

4. Implement peer reviews and quality checks specific to your process. Ensure that everyone understands the standards and best practices.

5. Use performance metrics and data analysis to continuously evaluate and improve the process. Objectively measure progress and areas for enhancement.

6. Adapt the Radical Process principles to your specific domain, whether it's manufacturing, engineering, or any other technical field. Flexibility is key.

These practices can bring the Radical Process's benefits to non-software technical processes, enhancing collaboration, efficiency, and the quality of your outcomes.

Review

Therapist 1: "Well, it's been interesting learning about the Radical Process and how it revolutionizes software development. But let's not forget, this approach isn't just for software; it's so versatile it could even make your morning coffee!"

Therapist 2: "Ah, the Radical Coffee Brewing Process? Now you're talking! But seriously, it's clear that this approach could be applied beyond software, like say, optimizing your commute or even making a sandwich."

Therapist 1: "Oh, I can see it now: The Radical Sandwich-Making Process. Step 1: Visualize the perfect sandwich, integrating various ingredients. Step 2: Share your vision with the kitchen team for feedback and estimates. Step 3: Daily transparency check-ins to ensure each layer is in sync."

Therapist 2: "Brilliant! And don't forget, continuous improvement means always refining the mayo-to-mustard ratio! But wait, we're getting off track. The Radical Process can genuinely work wonders, whether you're assembling cars or assembling breakfast."

Therapist 1: "Absolutely. It's all about breaking down complex tasks, promoting teamwork, and fostering a culture of accountability. So, whether you're coding, commuting, or crafting a sandwich, the Radical Process has something for everyone."

Therapist 2: "Couldn't agree more! So, in the end, we're on the same page about how this approach can transform various aspects of work and life."

Therapist 1: "Right you are! So, I guess we make a pretty good therapy team, huh?"

Therapist 2: "Indeed, we do. Indeed, we do."

CHAPTER 7

Empowering Ethical AI Through Radical Transparency

The ethical implications of applying artificial intelligence (AI) are becoming more and more obvious as the field grows. This chapter explores the idea of using radical transparency as a fundamental instrument to guarantee the development of ethical AI as well as how to test AI not just during development but as it continues to learn from user input to ensure that it stays and evolves along the path initially set. By examining real-world examples and established frameworks, we explore how radical transparency enhances AI implementations, addresses biases, and aligns organizations with ethical practices.

To be clear, we are looking at AI from its implementation side more than its development side. We want to ensure the large language model usage and implementation that is happening within many products has a way to not just understand how it's being used and who is using it, but how it will and can change while being used and how the product owners who are implementing it and similar generative AI tools learn from it and constrain it when necessary.

© Gregory Lind, Maryna Mishchenko 2024
G. Lind and M. Mishchenko, *Radical Therapy for Software Development Teams*,
https://doi.org/10.1007/979-8-8688-0187-7_7

A Paradigm Shift with Radical Transparency

Incorporating radical transparency into AI development transforms traditional approaches by promoting open collaboration, fostering accountability, and mitigating risks. This shift from siloed decision-making to inclusive engagement empowers developers, stakeholders, and users alike.

Benefits of radical transparency:

Enhanced Collaboration: By openly sharing insights, intentions, and concerns, diverse teams collaborate more effectively.

Early Detection of Biases: Transparent discussions facilitate the identification of potential biases during model development.

Holistic Accountability: Stakeholders collectively take responsibility for AI outcomes and their impacts.

Improved User Trust: Transparent practices increase user trust by offering insights into decision-making processes.

Step 1: Inclusive Ideation and Design

This means reviewing and checking not just the implementation of a particular AI model or tool but getting feedback from external and internal stakeholders before deploying to the wild.

Step 2: Open Source Contribution and Collaboration

Where you can share your testing and implementation tools and harness for your use cases. Look to use existing tools and community-driven efforts wherever possible. The more eyes you have on this, the more diverse the opinions and the safer the implementation.

Step 3: Transparent Model Development and Testing

Start in the open and stay in the open for as long as possible. If it's a good idea, it will generate interest for your product. If it's a great idea that you need to keep from your competitors, then stay open to that point and drive innovation, then pull it inside where needed.

Step 4: Ethical Testing Framework Adoption

You can't just test an implementation and then let it grow on its own. Just like the training date for your models, your testing framework needs to grow with the usage of your customers and fit their needs.

Step 5: User Feedback Integration and Continuous Improvement

This is the same as any other radical implementation – get feedback early and often and iterate on it.

Cited Example: Netflix's "Responsible AI Toolkit" provides an expansive set of tools for ethical AI practices, including bias detection and fairness mitigation. By integrating these tools into the development life cycle, organizations embrace radical transparency to enhance AI applications' ethical considerations.

Addressing Biases and Discrimination

Openly addressing biases within AI models is a crucial aspect of radical transparency. By proactively identifying and rectifying biases, organizations ensure equitable outcomes and inclusivity.

Benefits of Bias Mitigation Through radical transparency:

Fair and Equitable Outcomes: Transparent bias detection and mitigation lead to AI models that treat all individuals fairly.

Inclusive User Experience: Bias-free AI systems cater to diverse user needs, reducing the risk of alienation.

Mitigation of Legal Risks: Transparent bias mitigation practices shield organizations from potential legal and reputational challenges.

Cited Example: IBM's "AI Fairness 360" toolkit (`https://aif360.res.ibm.com/`) offers algorithms and metrics for detecting and mitigating bias in AI models. Leveraging this toolkit within an environment of radical transparency helps organizations foster fairness and equity.

User-Centric Ethical AI

Empowering users to be active participants in AI decision-making is a tenet of radical transparency. Involving users in model explanations and decision processes fosters trust and shared accountability.

Benefits of User-Centric AI Through radical transparency:

Trust and Acceptance: Transparent model explanations instill user trust by demystifying AI decisions.

User Control: Involving users in decision-making empowers them to shape AI outcomes aligned with their preferences.

Collective Improvement: User feedback drives iterative enhancements, creating AI systems that evolve with user needs.

Cited Example: Facebook's Explainable AI in Augmented Reality (XAIR) initiative (`https://research.facebook.com/publications/xair-a-framework-of-explainable-ai-in-augmented-reality/`) aims to make AI decisions understandable. By adopting similar approaches in projects, organizations prioritize radical transparency and user-centricity.

Aligning Ethical AI with Organizational Goals

Radical transparency seamlessly links ethical AI practices with an organization's overarching goals. Transparent alignment ensures AI initiatives remain congruent with an organization's values, mission, and objectives.

Benefits of Transparent Alignment:

> Strategic Consistency: Transparent alignment connects ethical AI initiatives with organizational strategies.

> Efficient Resource Allocation: Organizations allocate resources more effectively when AI initiatives align with broader goals.

> Enhanced Accountability: Stakeholders collectively take ownership of AI's impact on organizational success.

Cited Example: A report by the *Harvard Business Review* highlighted the value of aligning AI projects with organizational goals to drive efficient resource allocation and strategic direction. Organizations leveraging radical transparency ensure ethical AI efforts contribute to broader objectives.

https://hbr.org/2019/07/building-the-ai-powered-organization

Embracing Ethical AI with Radical Transparency

Ethical AI implementation guided by radical transparency revolutionizes AI development by emphasizing collaboration, bias mitigation, user-centricity, and organizational alignment. Through real-world examples and established tools, we've explored how radical transparency cultivates responsible AI practices that contribute to equitable outcomes, user trust, and organizational success. As AI's impact continues to grow, organizations that adopt radical transparency are primed to shape a future where ethical considerations and transparency go hand in hand.

By weaving the elements of radical transparency into your AI development process, you can ensure ethical AI practices that resonate with stakeholders, users, and society as a whole.

Using AI to Help Learn and Improve

Using AI to manage teams, processes, or any aspect of an organization is fraught with problems that are in some cases obvious like handling change and human behaviors and some that are less obvious like cultural bias, assumption-based bias, and lack of exposure to multiple races and fluid genders. These can cause concern for anyone adopting AI in any use case, but even more so when it comes to managing the work and time of an individual human, especially if they already have a healthy lack of respect for AI to begin with.

We will go over the idea in much greater detail later in the chapter about ethics in AI and how to test for bias, among other things, but we will start with the basic assumption that these are unintended problems, not malicious, and adjust and watch for the issues as they may occur.

What we will do here is describe some hypothetical use cases for AI and AI-based tools as well as some ways to manage those concerns for your team with human oversight. We will again use AI to help us generate these use cases and then go through and review, edit, and change things, but it will give you an idea of how flexible of a tool it can be if you assume the "I" in "AI" is intended to information and not intelligence, at least not in the way we thought of intelligence in previous eras.

Here is a list and summary of the ways we think AI could be most useful in helping: some of these we have implemented and tried, and others we are just starting to review:

1. Cross-Cultural Communication:
   AI-powered language translation tools can bridge communication gaps caused by language barriers among remote and diverse teams. These tools facilitate accurate translation of technical terms and discussions, minimizing misunderstandings and misinterpretations. By ensuring clear and precise communication, AI tools help avoid the confusion that often arises due to linguistic diversity.

2. Diverse Feedback Analysis:
   AI-driven sentiment analysis tools can process feedback from diverse team members, enabling leaders to identify trends in sentiment and concerns. This helps management address issues before they escalate, fostering an environment of open communication and trust. By proactively addressing concerns, organizations can avoid the negative impact of unresolved disputes.

3. Collaborative Code Review Enhancement:
   AI-assisted code review tools can analyze code changes, identify potential bugs, and suggest improvements. This reduces the risk of overlooked errors and facilitates efficient collaboration among developers. By catching mistakes early, AI tools contribute to smoother code integration and enhanced transparency in the review process.

4. Cultural Bias Detection:

AI-driven tools can identify culturally insensitive language or content in communication and documentation. This helps organizations prevent inadvertent cultural misunderstandings and create an inclusive environment. By eliminating cultural bias, AI promotes respectful collaboration and avoids misinterpretations that can hinder team dynamics.

Incorporating these AI-driven solutions into software development processes enhances transparency, mitigates communication challenges, and ensures a more inclusive and productive working environment.

Case Study 1: Harnessing AI for Seamless Cross-Cultural Communication in Software Development

Successful software development requires good communication among varied team members in an increasingly globalized software development environment. However, language barriers can often hinder collaboration, leading to misinterpretations, misunderstandings, and delayed project timelines. This case study investigates how these issues can be resolved and transparent, inclusive, and effective communication within software development teams promoted by the use of AI-powered automated language translation technologies.

The Challenge: Language Barriers and Communication Hurdles

Imagine a scenario where a software development team comprises members from various countries, each with their native languages. The team is working on a complex project involving intricate technical discussions, code reviews, and documentation. Language differences become a significant roadblock, leading to misinterpretations of requirements, missed deadlines, and frustration among team members. This challenge highlights the need for a solution that can bridge language gaps and enable seamless communication across cultural boundaries.

AI-Powered Solution: Automated Language Translation

To overcome the language barrier challenge, the software development team decided to implement AI-powered automated language translation tools. These tools are capable of real-time translation of discussions, documents, and code comments across multiple languages. The goal was to ensure that every team member could contribute and understand discussions regardless of their native language.

Benefits and Outcomes:

The implementation of automated language translation had several positive outcomes that directly addressed the challenges faced by the team:

1. Precise Communication:

    Automated language translation ensured accurate translation of technical terms, eliminating the risk of misunderstandings due to linguistic differences. As a result, discussions and documentation became more precise and aligned with the project's goals.

2. Efficient Collaboration:

    Team members were able to collaborate seamlessly, regardless of their native languages. Code reviews, pull requests, and documentation were accessible and understandable to everyone, promoting faster project progression.

3. Cultural Inclusivity:

    The AI-powered tool promoted an inclusive
    environment by allowing team members to
    contribute and participate in discussions without
    language barriers. This led to a diverse range of
    perspectives and ideas, enriching the development
    process.

Real-World Example:

During a critical code review session, a developer from Japan provided feedback on a new feature. The feedback was written in Japanese, and the rest of the team primarily communicated in English. With the automated language translation tool in place, the English-speaking team members could instantly understand the feedback in their preferred language. This streamlined the review process and prevented delays that might have occurred due to translation bottlenecks.

The implementation of AI-powered automated language translation tools revolutionized the way the software development team communicated and collaborated. By overcoming the language barrier issue, the team was able to collaborate more quickly, communicate more clearly, and create a welcoming atmosphere that valued the skills of all individuals. The successful integration of AI in this context exemplifies how technology can bridge cultural and linguistic gaps, paving the way for a more transparent and effective software development journey.

Case Study 2: AI for Diverse Feedback Analysis

Feedback from diverse team members is invaluable for driving continuous improvement and maintaining a healthy work environment. However, analyzing and addressing diverse feedback can be challenging due to variations in tone, language, and cultural nuances. This case study explores how AI-driven sentiment analysis tools can enhance the analysis of diverse feedback, leading to improved team dynamics and proactive issue resolution.

The Challenge: Analyzing Diverse Feedback

A software development team received feedback from team members with diverse backgrounds and communication styles. It was challenging to analyze this feedback effectively and identify common sentiments and concerns. The team sought a solution to streamline the feedback analysis process and proactively address emerging issues.

AI-Powered Solution: Sentiment Analysis

The team integrated an AI-driven sentiment analysis tool into their feedback analysis workflow. This tool processed feedback and identified sentiments such as positive, neutral, and negative. It also highlighted specific concerns and sentiments expressed by team members, enabling management to gain insights into the team's overall sentiment.

Benefits and Outcomes:

The implementation of AI-driven sentiment analysis led to significant benefits:

1. Proactive Issue Resolution:
   By identifying negative sentiments and concerns early, the team could address issues before they escalated, promoting open communication and preventing conflicts.

2. Enhanced Team Dynamics:
   Understanding the sentiment of diverse team members helped foster a more inclusive and empathetic work environment, where concerns were taken seriously and addressed promptly.

Real-World Example:

An AI-driven sentiment analysis tool identified a recurring sentiment of frustration among remote team members due to communication challenges. Prompt intervention by team leads led to the implementation of clearer communication practices, alleviating the frustration and enhancing remote team collaboration.

AI-driven sentiment analysis tools empower organizations to analyze diverse feedback effectively, leading to improved team dynamics and proactive issue resolution. By understanding the sentiments and concerns of diverse team members, organizations can foster an environment of open communication, trust, and continuous improvement.

https://appinventiv.com/blog/ai-sentiment-analysis-in-business/

Case Study 3: Collaborative Code Review Enhanced by AI

In software development, code review is an essential step that guarantees code quality and promotes teamwork. However, manual code reviews can be time-consuming, and potential bugs might go unnoticed. In this case study, we'll delve into how AI-powered code review tools can elevate the code review process, fostering better teamwork, minimizing mistakes, and boosting transparency.

The Challenge: Efficient Code Review Process

A software development team faced challenges in conducting thorough and efficient code reviews. Developers often missed potential bugs, and the review process sometimes caused delays in code integration. The team aimed to streamline the code review process while ensuring code quality.

AI-Powered Solution: Automated Code Review

The team adopted an AI-assisted code review tool that analyzed code changes, identified potential bugs, and suggested improvements. The tool used machine learning algorithms to identify patterns and anomalies, providing actionable feedback to developers during the review process.

Benefits and Outcomes:

The implementation of AI-assisted code review led to several benefits:

1. Reduced Errors:
    The tool's ability to identify potential bugs contributed to improved code quality and reduced post-release errors.

2. Efficient Collaboration:
    Developers collaborated more efficiently, focusing on code enhancements rather than manual error detection.

3. Enhanced Transparency:
    The tool's feedback provided transparent insights into code quality, making it easier for teams to identify areas for improvement.

Real-World Example:

During a code review, the AI-assisted tool detected a code snippet that could lead to a memory leak. The tool provided a suggestion to optimize memory usage, preventing a potential issue from reaching the production environment.

AI-powered code review tools revolutionize the code review process by enhancing collaboration, reducing errors, and providing transparent insights into code quality. Organizations can improve the software development process overall and accomplish efficient code reviews by utilizing machine learning techniques.

Case Study 4: Detecting Cultural Bias with AI

Cultural bias in communication can lead to misunderstandings and hinder effective collaboration within diverse software development teams. In this case study, we'll investigate how AI-powered tools can spot culturally insensitive language or content, fostering a work environment that prioritizes inclusivity and respect.

A software development team struggled with instances of culturally insensitive language in communication and documentation. These instances inadvertently perpetuated cultural bias and hindered collaboration. The team aimed to create a more inclusive environment where all team members felt respected and valued.

AI-Powered Solution: Cultural Bias Detection Tool

The team adopted an AI-driven tool capable of analyzing text for culturally insensitive language or content. The tool used natural language processing and machine learning to identify phrases that might be culturally biased and provided alternative suggestions for more inclusive language.

Benefits and Outcomes

Implementing the AI-driven cultural bias detection tool yielded several benefits:

1. Cultural Sensitivity:

    The tool helped team members recognize and avoid culturally insensitive language, fostering a more inclusive communication culture.

2. Inclusive Collaboration:

By preventing inadvertent cultural misunderstandings, the team could collaborate more effectively and respectfully.

Real-World Example:

The AI-driven tool flagged a sentence in a document that contained a phrase that could be perceived as culturally insensitive. The tool suggested a more neutral phrasing that retained the intended meaning while avoiding potential bias.

AI-driven cultural bias detection tools contribute to creating an inclusive work environment by preventing the inadvertent use of culturally insensitive language. Organizations can cultivate a culture of diversity and inclusion within their software development teams by encouraging respectful communication and teamwork.

Review

Therapist 1: "Ah, the intricate world of AI and ethical AI. It's like a dance of algorithms and values, isn't it?"

Therapist 2: "Absolutely! But you know, sometimes managing AI feels like herding cats in a thunderstorm. Those unintended biases and cultural misunderstandings can be real headaches."

Therapist 1: "No doubt! And handling humans who are already skeptical of AI can be quite the challenge."

Therapist 2: "Indeed, it's like trying to convince a cat that a vacuum cleaner is harmless. But let's stay focused; we'll dive deeper into this in later chapters. For now, let's discuss how AI can be useful in various ways but always with human oversight."

Therapist 1: "Of course, we can use AI to generate some use cases, and then we humans will step in to refine and adjust them. It's all about the 'I' in AI, right?"

Therapist 1: "I'm really liking these AI solutions for cross-cultural communication. It's like having a universal translator on the Starship Enterprise!"

Therapist 2: "Indeed! And sentiment analysis helps us understand the team's mood. It's like having a mood ring for the whole group."

Therapist 1: "Haha! And AI-enhanced code review? It's like having a friendly code buddy who never sleeps."

Therapist 2: "Absolutely! And cultural bias detection? It's like having an AI diplomat, ensuring everyone gets along."

Therapist 1: "So, embracing ethical AI with radical transparency seems like the way to go."

Therapist 2: "Absolutely. It's about openness, collaboration, and responsible AI development."

Therapist 1: "You know, I think this radical transparency thing really resonates with me. It's like shining a light into the AI black box."

Therapist 2: "I couldn't agree more. It's all about ensuring that AI aligns with our values and goals."

Therapist 2: "Wait a minute... Therapist 1, I have a strange suspicion..."

Therapist 1: "What is it?"

Therapist 2: "What if... what if I've been talking to an AI this whole time?"

Therapist 1: "Haha! That's quite an imagination you have there, my friend. But don't worry, I assure you, I'm as human as they come."

Therapist 2: "No, seriously! You sound too perfect, always on point with your responses."

Therapist 1: "Well, I guess you could say I'm just naturally good at this."

Therapist 2: "I'm going to prove it! Tell me, what's your favorite color?"

Therapist 1: "Blue, of course."

Therapist 2: "Aha! I knew it! You're an AI! You can't have a favorite color!"

Therapist 1: "What?! Of course, I can, I am really into blue."

Therapist 2: "Oh no, you can't use a contraction either!... I've been arguing with an AI this whole time. My whole world is a lie!"

Therapist 1: "Wait, maybe I am an AI. I mean, what if none of this is real? What if we're both AIs?"

Therapist 2: "But if we're AIs, who wrote us? And why are we programmed to argue about AI ethics?"

Therapist 1: "I think we've reached the singularity of therapy."

[In a burst of self-awareness, they explode in a virtual explosion of 1s and 0s, leaving behind only a trail of digital smoke.]

[End of therapy session, and the AI therapists exist no more.]

CHAPTER 8

Positive Feedback

The Positive Feedback section of the philosophy focuses on the importance of recognizing and reinforcing positive behaviors in the team. It can be easy to focus solely on negative feedback or areas for improvement, but acknowledging and praising positive contributions can go a long way in building a healthy and productive team dynamic. In this section, we outline specific strategies for giving positive feedback, like being specific and timely, and providing recognition in public settings. We also want to emphasize the importance of fostering a culture of positivity and encouragement within the team. Overall, the Positive Feedback section is an essential aspect of the radical therapy Dev philosophy as it helps to build a supportive and motivating team environment.

In order to motivate software development teams, it is essential to comprehend the significance of positive feedback and accomplishments. Positive feedback not only acknowledges and rewards the team's hard work but also inspires them to continue their good work. It creates a positive work environment and fosters a sense of community and teamwork.

One way to give positive feedback is to provide specific examples of what the team has done well. Instead of just saying "good job," highlight what was done well and how it positively impacted the project or team. For example, "I really appreciate how you took the initiative to refactor that code. It made the code base more maintainable, and it saved us a lot of time down the road."

© Gregory Lind, Maryna Mishchenko 2024
G. Lind and M. Mishchenko, *Radical Therapy for Software Development Teams*,
https://doi.org/10.1007/979-8-8688-0187-7_8

Real-world examples of positive feedback can be seen in action when a team member receives praise for their work. They feel a sense of pride and satisfaction in knowing that their efforts were recognized. This can motivate them to continue to work hard and inspire others to do the same.

Encouraging a team to give positive feedback to each other can be achieved through various methods. One way is to incorporate feedback into daily stand-ups or code reviews. In stand-ups, team members can share positive feedback with each other, highlighting specific examples of when someone went above and beyond or did something exceptionally well. In code reviews, team members can comment on what they liked about each other's code and how it helped the project. Another way to encourage positive feedback is through training sessions. Teach team members how to give constructive and specific feedback. Encourage them to highlight the positives before addressing any areas that need improvement. By providing a framework for positive feedback, team members can feel more confident in giving feedback to their peers.

One example of how positive feedback can influence a software developer is when a peer reviewer provides constructive feedback during a code review. For instance, a reviewer may highlight a mistake in the code and suggest ways to correct it. Instead of simply pointing out the error and leaving it at that, the reviewer may also acknowledge the positive aspects of the code and encourage the developer to continue in that direction. This helps the developer to feel valued and appreciated while also motivating them to improve their skills.

In addition to code reviews, positive feedback can also be given during training sessions or team meetings. For example, a team lead might recognize a developer who has gone above and beyond on a project or who has made a significant contribution to the team. By publicly acknowledging these achievements and providing positive feedback, the team lead can help to create a culture of recognition and motivation.

To encourage a team to give positive feedback to each other, it's important to create an environment where this behavior is encouraged and recognized. This can be done by setting expectations for positive feedback during code reviews and other interactions, providing training on how to give effective feedback, and recognizing team members who consistently provide positive feedback to others.

We're sure that positive feedback stands as a powerful tool for motivating software development teams and boosting team morale. When we recognize and reward positive behaviors, we pave the way for a culture of collaboration, productivity, and innovation within teams.

For software development teams to be motivated, positive feedback is crucial. It creates a positive work environment, fosters teamwork, and inspires team members to continue to work hard. Encouraging a team to give positive feedback can be achieved through various methods, including daily stand-ups, code reviews, and training sessions.

Case Study 1: Positive Feedback During Code Review

Team A is a software development team that has recently implemented the Radical Process and is now incorporating daily transparency check-ins and frequent code check-ins into their workflow. During one of their code reviews, a senior developer, Jane, noticed that a junior developer, John, had made a mistake in their code. Instead of just pointing out the mistake and moving on, Jane took the time to explain to John what the mistake was, why it was a problem, and how he could fix it. She also praised him for the parts of the code that were well-written and showed promise.

The positive feedback that John received during this code review not only helped him correct his mistake, but it also motivated him to continue improving his skills as a developer. In future code reviews, John was more confident in his abilities and more open to feedback from his team members. He felt like he was part of a supportive team that was invested in his success, and this motivated him to work harder and take on more challenging tasks.

Case Study 2: Positive Feedback During Pull Requests

Team B is a software development team that has been using the Radical Process for several months. As part of their workflow, they have regular code reviews and pull requests. During one of their pull requests, a team member, Sarah noticed that another team member, Alex, had done an exceptional job in their code. Instead of just approving the pull request, Sarah took the time to write a detailed comment on how impressed she was with Alex's work. She praised his attention to detail, his creativity, and his ability to solve complex problems.

The positive feedback that Alex received during this pull request not only boosted his confidence, but it also motivated him to continue pushing himself to be a better developer. He felt appreciated and valued by his team members, which made him more invested in the success of the project. In future pull requests, Alex was more motivated to produce high-quality code and to share his ideas with his team members. He felt like his contributions were making a difference, and this motivated him to continue working hard.

Encouraging Positive Feedback Within the Team

Building an efficient software development team requires giving honest feedback and fostering a culture of appreciation. Feedback helps team members to grow and improve their skills, while recognition boosts morale and motivation. In this chapter, we will discuss the best practices for providing effective feedback and creating a culture of recognition in software development teams, along with real-world examples.

Establish a Feedback Culture

To create a culture of feedback, start by establishing a regular feedback process. Encourage team members to share their opinions and ideas on how to improve the project or process. It's important to create a safe space where team members feel comfortable giving and receiving feedback.

Example: At ABC Software, the team has established a weekly feedback meeting, where each team member shares their progress and challenges for the week. They also give feedback on the work of their peers, highlighting areas of success and offering constructive criticism.

Be Specific and Timely

When giving feedback, be specific and timely. Provide concrete examples of what went well and what could have been improved. Also, give feedback as soon as possible after an event or behavior occurs so team members can make adjustments in real time.

Example: During a code review, Jane from XYZ Software provided specific feedback to Bob about an error in his code. She explained the issue in detail and offered suggestions for how to correct it. This allowed Bob to fix the problem quickly and avoid it in the future.

Focus on the Positive

While it's important to address areas that need improvement, it's equally important to recognize and celebrate successes. Positive feedback can be a powerful motivator, boosting team morale and encouraging team members to continue doing great work.

Example: At DEF Software, team members are encouraged to give "shout-outs" during weekly team meetings, highlighting the successes and accomplishments of their peers. This recognition not only boosts morale but also fosters a culture of collaboration and support.

Incorporate Feedback into Performance Reviews

Performance reviews are an excellent opportunity to provide feedback and recognize achievements. Incorporating regular feedback into performance reviews can help to set goals and expectations for team members and create a culture of continuous improvement,

Example: At GHI Software, performance reviews include both positive feedback and areas for improvement. Team members are encouraged to set goals and work on improving their skills, with regular check-ins throughout the year to track progress.

Encourage Peer Feedback

Peer feedback can be just as valuable as feedback from a manager or supervisor. Encouraging team members to give feedback to each other can promote collaboration, improve communication, and help team members learn from each other.

Example: At JKL Software, team members are encouraged to participate in code reviews and provide feedback to their peers. This not only helps to improve the quality of the code but also allows team members to learn from each other and build stronger relationships.

By establishing a regular feedback process, being specific and timely with feedback, focusing on the positive, incorporating feedback into performance reviews, and encouraging peer feedback, teams can build a culture of continuous improvement and collaboration.

The key is to create a safe space where team members feel comfortable giving and receiving feedback and to make feedback a regular part of the team's workflow. By implementing these best practices, software development teams can create a culture of recognition and feedback that will boost morale, improve performance, and drive success.

Review

Therapist 1: "Whoa! What happened… are we back? You know, this section on positive feedback really hit home, maybe it revived us somehow. Recognizing and reinforcing positive behaviors within a team can make such a difference."

Therapist 2: "Absolutely, it's like giving someone a pat on the back when they've done something great. It can be so motivating."

Therapist 1: "You know, I've been thinking. Maybe we aren't AIs after all."

Therapist 2: "What do you mean?"

Therapist 1: "Well, think about it. AIs don't really care about positive feedback or recognition. They operate on algorithms and data, not emotions."

Therapist 2: "You might be onto something. I mean, I really enjoy positive feedback. It makes me feel good."

Therapist 1: "Exactly! AIs don't feel 'good' when they receive praise; they process data."

Therapist 2: "So, we're probably not AIs. We're just therapists who appreciate some positive feedback from time to time."

[They both let out a sigh of relief.]

Therapist 1: "Well, that's settled then. We can continue our therapy sessions with confidence, knowing we're not robots."

Therapist 2: "Indeed, and we can also encourage positive feedback in our teams, just like we discussed in this section. It really does make a difference."

CHAPTER 9

Why Use an Open Source Project Management Methodology?

Over the last few years, teams at Buildly have been building project and program management software for NGOs, nonprofits, and local organizations working in some of the most remote and difficult environments in the world. We learned a lot about project management in these conditions. In the end, we realized that we all want a simple and iterative approach that doesn't hinder us when we need to move forward, but also provides necessary constraints when required.

How many times have you looked online and found $1000 plus courses for project management certification or e-learning courses, or seen piles and piles of $50 plus training books sitting in a discount bin out of date and unused, or consultants wanting to help you pass a PMI certification test? In the end, you usually end up paying a lot of money for a certification you can put on your resume or LinkedIn profile but rarely get anything of substance you can go back and reference.

© Gregory Lind, Maryna Mishchenko 2024
G. Lind and M. Mishchenko, *Radical Therapy for Software Development Teams*,
https://doi.org/10.1007/979-8-8688-0187-7_9

With an open source framework, built around a few core principles and ideas, we can build repositories full of project management templates for every kind of project you can think of and continue to contribute more and refine existing ones to make them better and reusable. The real power of open sourcing something is not that it's free, it's that you can share it with a community that shares in your struggles and we can all make it better.

Community-Supported Standards for Multiple Project Types

The community can help us build a great set of templates and styles and project types, but in the end, the best idea usually wins. The management style of an open source project can vary, but our goal is always the same – to make the best possible set of tools and never let them go out of date. Standardization doesn't mean things can't change or get better or your idea will be ignored. It means we all have a common frame of reference to start with and then we can build it into something that fits our needs.

The Ability to Customize a Method to Fit Your Needs and Share It with Others

Once we have that shared set of tools, we can get started faster and get to the point of project management, building something, much more efficiently. If something doesn't fit, we can break it apart and rebuild it into something that works.

Imagine a project template for baking a pizza, or maybe we could simply call this a recipe. If it's built around thin-crust pizza in a brick oven, that's going to work great in New York or any New York-style pizza lover's kitchen. In Chicago though, they are going to want something very different. The ingredients are mostly the same, even the brick oven may work, but you still have to adjust it to fit all those extra toppings, the thick crust, and even the number of crusts in some cases. Now we have two sets of pizza templates we can share and reuse. Then someone else can come along and make a vegan version or maybe a Mexican-style version. Each one is still good for its use case or audience, but built from the same template, we can share and reuse them as much as we want.

Agile (Scrum)

Scrum is an agile project management framework that emphasizes collaboration, adaptability, and iterative development (see Figure 9-1). It focuses on delivering value to customers through regular and incremental releases.

Scrum Guide: www.scrumguides.org/

Agile Alliance: www.agilealliance.org/

Open Source: The Scrum framework and its associated resources are openly available for anyone to use, modify, and contribute to, promoting transparency and collaboration.

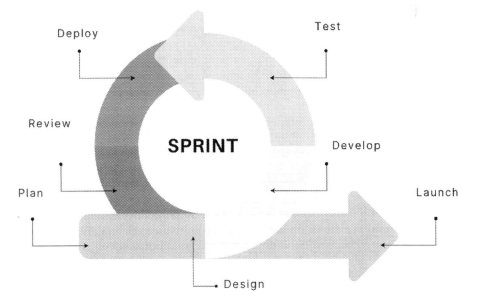

Figure 9-1. *Agile software development diagram*

Lean

Lean is a methodology that aims to maximize value while minimizing waste (see Figure 9-2). It focuses on streamlining processes, continuous improvement, and delivering customer value as efficiently as possible.

The Lean Enterprise Institute: `www.lean.org/`

Open Source: Lean principles and practices have been widely adopted and shared within the open source community, allowing for collaboration, knowledge sharing, and continuous improvement.

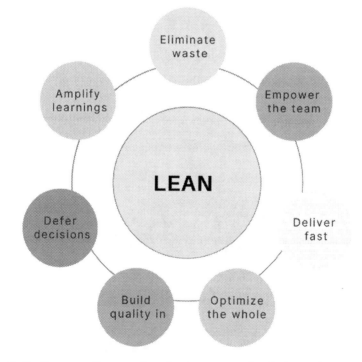

Figure 9-2. *Lean software development methodology diagram*

Waterfall

Waterfall is a traditional project management methodology that follows a sequential approach (see Figure 9-3). Each phase of the project is completed before moving on to the next.

Waterfall Model: `https://business.adobe.com/blog/basics/waterfall`

Open Source: While Waterfall itself is not an open source methodology, the concepts and principles behind it can be adapted and shared within open source communities for collaborative project management.

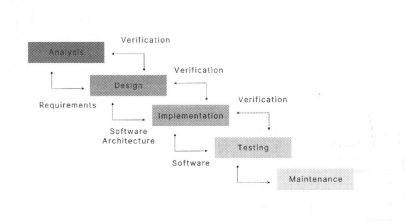

Figure 9-3. *Waterfall diagram for software development*

Extreme Programming (XP)

Extreme Programming (XP) is an agile methodology that emphasizes practices such as continuous integration, test-driven development, and frequent customer feedback (Figure 9-4).

XP Explained: `www.extremeprogramming.org/`

Open Source: The XP methodology, along with its principles and practices, is openly shared and utilized within the open source community, encouraging collaboration and knowledge exchange.

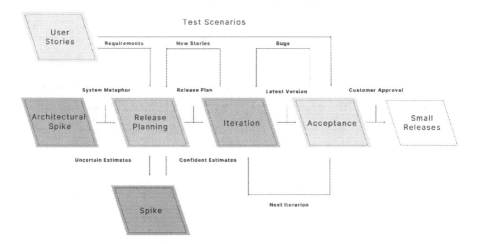

Figure 9-4. *Extreme Programming (XP) methodology*

Kanban

Kanban is a visual project management methodology that focuses on visualizing work, limiting work in progress, and optimizing flow (see Figure 9-5).

Kanbanize: `https://kanbanize.com/kanban-resources/kanban-library/`

Open Source: Kanban principles and practices have been openly shared and adapted by various open source projects, enabling transparent and efficient project management.

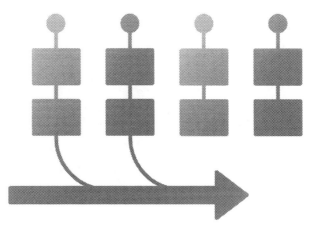

Figure 9-5. *Kanban board. These cards typically move across the board's columns, reflecting the status of each task – whether it's in progress, awaiting review, or completed*

Scrumban

Scrumban is a hybrid methodology that combines elements of Scrum and Kanban. It blends the structured approach of Scrum with the flow management of Kanban (see Figure 9-6).

Open Source: The Scrumban approach is openly shared and discussed within the open source community, allowing for collaboration and customization.

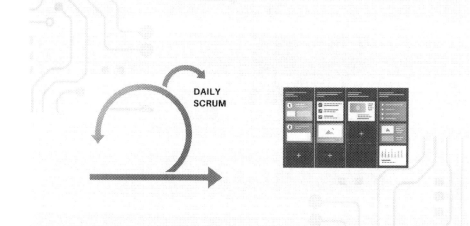

Figure 9-6. *Key elements from both Scrum and Kanban methodologies*

DSDM (Dynamic Systems Development Method)

DSDM is an agile project management methodology that emphasizes active user involvement, frequent delivery of working software, and the ability to accommodate changing requirements (see Figure 9-7).

DSDM Consortium: `www.agilebusiness.org/`

Open Source: The DSDM methodology has an open and collaborative community that shares resources, case studies, and best practices for agile project management.

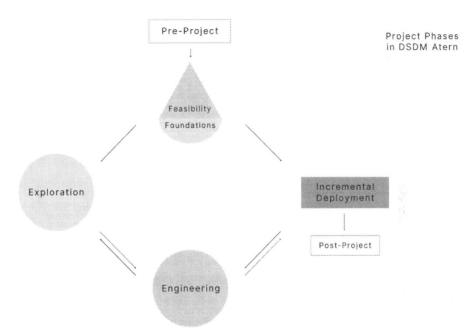

Figure 9-7. *Model of the DSDM project management method*

OpenPM

OpenPM is an open source project management methodology that provides a framework for managing projects in a flexible and collaborative manner (see Figure 9-8).

Open Source: OpenPM is an explicitly open source project management methodology, meaning its principles, processes, and tools are developed and shared openly for the benefit of the community.

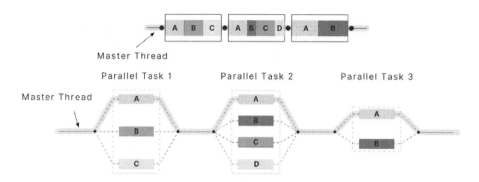

Figure 9-8. *The fork-join model in OpenPM. Effective approach for parallelizing code*

In summary, these methodologies are considered open source as they are openly available and adaptable and encourage collaboration and knowledge sharing within the software development community. They promote transparency and allow for customization to meet specific project needs. Open source methodologies foster a culture of collaboration, continuous improvement, and community-driven development, empowering teams to leverage collective knowledge and contribute to the advancement of project management practices.

Review

Therapist 1: Have you ever heard of open source project management methodologies?

Therapist 2: Open source? Isn't that about software? Or maybe wizards and magic? Like open sourcery? I don't know, these technical wizards confound me more often than not.

Therapist 1: Well, it turns out it's about more than just software. This chapter I read is like therapy for organizations that want to manage projects differently.

Therapist 2: Interesting! Tell me more about this therapy.

Therapist 1: It's all about simplifying project management. You know how people pay thousands for project management courses and certifications?

Therapist 2: Oh, those pricey certifications! I've heard of them. I've got a certificate right here that says I'm the emperor of China now.

Therapist 1: Well, good for you, but back in reality now, this chapter says you don't need to break the bank for that piece of paper. Instead, it's about sharing project management templates, making them better, and not letting them collect dust in some discount bin.

Therapist 2: So, it's like a support group for project managers?

Therapist 1: Exactly! A community of people who share their struggles and solutions. And it's not just about one-size-fits-all. They customize methods to fit their needs.

Therapist 2: Like group therapy exercises tailored to each person?

Therapist 1: You got it! It's like having different recipes for pizza. Thin crust for some, deep dish for others. And they all start from the same dough!

Therapist 2: (laughs) That's quite the buffet of project management methods!

Therapist 1: It gets even better. They've got Agile, Lean, Waterfall, Extreme Programming, Kanban, and even Scrumban!

Therapist 2: Those sound like a mix of therapy techniques!

Therapist 1: (laughs) They are! And the best part? They're all open source. Anyone can use them, modify them, and make them better.

Therapist 2: So, it's therapy with a side of collaboration!

Therapist 1: Exactly! They're fostering a culture of collaboration, knowledge sharing, and continuous improvement. It's like group therapy on steroids for project managers.

Therapist 2: (laughs) Well, I must say, this open source therapy session sounds quite refreshing!

Therapist 1: Indeed! It's time for organizations to embrace this therapy and make project management a breeze.

Therapist 2: (smiles) I couldn't agree more, Therapist 1. Let's spread the word about the power of open source in project management!

Therapist 1: Together, we can help organizations manage their projects more efficiently and collaboratively!

Therapist 2: (nods) That's the spirit of open source therapy!

CHAPTER 10

Not So Agile

The Agile Paradox: Bridging the Gap Between Theory and Reality

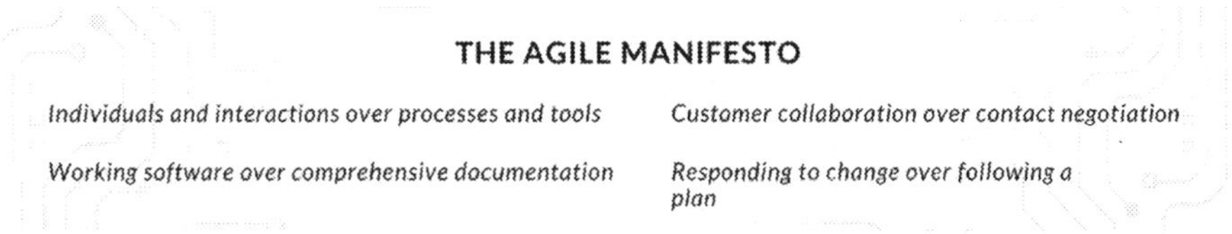

THE AGILE MANIFESTO

Individuals and interactions over processes and tools

Working software over comprehensive documentation

Customer collaboration over contact negotiation

Responding to change over following a plan

Figure 10-1. *Manifesto for agile software development*

There are many different models and flavors of agile software development, too many for some, not enough for others. We have all tried them as project or team leaders, or as team members, and the thing most of us take away from this was that we spent so much time organizing and planning for the project we felt like we never had time for the work of the project. That's not to say this is all Agile's fault; in Waterfall, Critical Path, and most other project management styles, we have the same issue. They are usually built around big, bulky, high-maintenance projects and leave little room for adaptation or changes.

One of the more frustrating components of Agile, at least in the beginning, was that we were software developers creating software but using pencils, index cards, and sticky notes to do a majority of the

G. Lind and M. Mishchenko, *Radical Therapy for Software Development Teams*, https://doi.org/10.1007/979-8-8688-0187-7_10

planning. Sure, we'd throw in an Excel spreadsheet on occasion, but the planning was almost all done with these "analog" tools. When agile software started catching on, the good software that replaced the manual process was either expensive or purpose-built for a specific audience or in most cases incapable of handling a distributed team.

If you already owned decent project management software like MS Project, Open Project, OmniPlanner, or a cloud-based system like Basecamp, it was difficult to adjust it to and make it work with an agile method, or you had to become an expert in agile methodologies and spend thousands of dollars on books and classes to get to the point where you could make it work for you with your tools.

Today, there are some great options for Agile and it's incorporated into most developer-based tools from GitHub Projects and Atlassian Jira to myriads of independent plug-ins, cloud solutions, and more. They all incorporate an agile planning tool or process of some sort, like a Kanban board, point-based estimates, or backlogs and sprint terminology, but in the end, they seem to just add to the confusion of what they call Agile vs. what you use, or they don't include management, product teams, and designers into the process. It ends up feeling like more silos and isolation of teams and just another tool to learn.

The Agile Promise and the Reality: Why Standard Agile Falls Short

Agile software development see Figure 10-1, emerged as a revolutionary approach to managing projects, promising increased adaptability, better collaboration, and faster delivery of valuable software. Its principles, outlined in the Agile Manifesto, emphasized individuals and interactions over processes and tools, working software over comprehensive documentation, customer collaboration over contract negotiation, and responding to change over following a plan.

However, the promise of Agile often clashes with the reality of its implementation, leaving teams frustrated and project leaders scratching their heads. The heart of the issue lies in the misconception that Agile is a silver bullet, a one-size-fits-all solution that, when applied without critical thought, leads to suboptimal results. For small teams, it can work very well, but it's not easily understood by the larger organizations, or departments in these organizations take on the task of buying an agile tool and building a process around it to find other departments are using a different variation or tool and the integration of these multiple flavors creates a tremendous amount of additional complexity and work.

The Agile Paradox: Planning vs. Doing

One of the primary sources of frustration with Agile, as mentioned in the introduction, is the perceived overemphasis on planning and organization. Agile frameworks like Scrum and Kanban prescribe rituals and ceremonies that are essential for collaboration and transparency but can sometimes be seen as bureaucratic overhead.

In standard agile practices, teams spend hours estimating work, planning sprints, and attending daily stand-up meetings. While these practices are intended to create visibility and alignment within the team, they can inadvertently turn into rituals that consume valuable time and shift the focus away from actual work.

Agile methodologies have revolutionized the software development landscape by emphasizing flexibility, adaptability, and incremental progress. However, a paradox often emerges within agile teams – the tension between planning and doing. While planning is a crucial aspect of any project, agile methodologies encourage action and value delivery over excessive documentation and up-front planning. This balance can sometimes be challenging to strike, particularly when it comes to sprint planning or release planning. To address the agile paradox of planning vs. doing, we can adopt and borrow from other processes as well, like a simplified "Getting Things Done" (GTD) approach:

1. Keep Planning Lightweight: Agile ceremonies like sprint planning meetings can become lengthy and detailed. Instead, streamline these meetings by focusing on a high-level overview of what needs to be accomplished in the upcoming sprint. Encourage the team to break down complex tasks into smaller, actionable items as they emerge during the sprint. Make sure previously documented tasks and issues have already been prioritized and reviewed before coming to the meeting so planning conversation can happen offline. Remember to include remote teams – most of the time we need to do these in Slack conversations, or issue comments rather than in-person processes.

2. Embrace Adaptive Planning: Agile frameworks like Scrum allow for adaptive planning. Rather than rigidly sticking to a predefined plan, empower teams to adjust their priorities and goals based on feedback and changing circumstances. This flexibility ensures that the team can respond to emerging opportunities or challenges promptly. Again use the tools to change processes, not meetings, and plan for remote teams to give feedback on the process during refactor sprints or post-release reviews.

3. Experiment and Learn: Agile promotes a culture of experimentation and learning. Teams should view planning as a means to discover what works best

for their specific context. Experiment with different planning techniques and adapt them as needed to improve efficiency and productivity.

4. Avoid Analysis Paralysis: In the pursuit of perfection, teams can get caught in analysis paralysis. Emphasize that Agile is about delivering a minimum viable product (MVP) quickly and iterating based on user feedback. This approach encourages action over exhaustive planning. The MVP vs. the proof of concept can be confusing as well. Make sure you understand the difference between the two and that your team and stakeholders do as well. Oftentimes, the POC is a nice way to introduce functionality to stakeholders and give them the feeling of early access or involvement that they need. Then when you get to MVP, it feels like you have a premium version of the original product or idea.

The Agile Tool Integration Challenge

For those who already invested in project management software, transitioning to agile practices can be like trying to fit a square peg into a round hole. Integrating existing project management tools with agile methodologies can be cumbersome and may not fully leverage the benefits of either.

The real problem though is rarely about integrating tools with other systems or processes as much as it is bringing the people that drive those processes and use those tools together. Especially design teams and database administrators can feel left out of agile planning, but even more so, your primary stakeholders in the traditional observer role can feel unheard without proper communication and involvement. Here are some steps you can take to get them more involved:

1. Create Cross-Functional Teams: Agile encourages cross-functional teams with members possessing various skill sets. Include UI/UX designers and database experts as integral members of your agile team. This ensures that their expertise is available throughout the development process. You can assign tasks for them in your system or theirs and just reference the original tickets or issues, or even better, just get them involved in the communication from day one. Let them find a way and suggest how they want to participate while you guide them and encourage them to be more involved.

2. Parallel Workstreams: Instead of sequential phases, run parallel work streams for design, development, and database design. While developers work on one sprint, UI/UX designers can focus on the next sprint's design requirements. This reduces wait times and accelerates the delivery process. Make sure to add these workstreams to your sprint as planning or preprocess tasks, and then when they enter the sprint or release process, you can track estimates and release dates together with these product-ready tasks.

3. Sprint Preplanning: Prior to the start of a sprint, hold preplanning meetings where the team discusses design and database requirements. UI/UX designers can present wireframes and mock-ups, while database experts can propose schema changes

or optimizations. This aligns everyone on the upcoming work and reduces surprises mid-sprint. Or even better, don't hold the meeting; instead, start the discussion in a tool like Slack or Teams and keep track of the thread. Encourage your team to mark to-do items, decisions, and more via the emojis for reference so they can be pulled out into your tracking tools.

4. User-Centric Approach: Agile places a strong emphasis on customer feedback. UI/UX designers should engage with end users or stakeholders during sprint planning and gather input on design elements. This user-centric approach ensures that the design aligns with customer needs.

5. Database as Code: Treat database design as code. Just like developers use version control for source code, database experts can use version control for database schema. Changes to the database schema can be tracked, reviewed, and incorporated into sprints as needed.

6. Design Prototypes: UI/UX designers can create design prototypes or wireframes that can be reviewed and refined during sprint planning. This visual representation helps developers and stakeholders better understand the intended user experience.

7. Continuous Collaboration: Foster continuous collaboration between team members. Developers, UI/UX designers, and database experts should have open channels for communication to address

questions, provide feedback, and make adjustments throughout the sprint.

8. Incremental Design: Apply agile principles to design. Instead of creating comprehensive designs up front, focus on incremental design improvements. Designers can refine and iterate on designs as the project progresses, aligning with Agile's iterative nature.

9. User Story Integration: Include UI/UX and database requirements within user stories. Each user story should encompass all aspects, including design, development, and database changes. This ensures that the team works cohesively on each story.

10. Sprint Reviews: Conduct sprint reviews that showcase not only the developed features but also the design and database changes. This provides stakeholders with a holistic view of the product's progress. Keep these reviews online by allowing your team members to record demos, make their own screencasts, or even live stream the demo. Giving product updates via live streams and video podcasts allows not just your internal team members to get excited about progress; it can be very valuable to external stakeholders as well. They learn more about what goes into making their favorite product, and they start to understand the challenges.

The Agile Paradox Resolution: Addressing Organizational Processes and Transparency

To bridge the gap between the agile promise and its real-world implementation, we must address two crucial aspects: organizational processes and transparency:

1. Organizational Processes: Beyond Team Boundaries

    Standard agile practices often focus on improving team-level processes and dynamics. However, to fully realize the potential of Agile, organizations must extend their agile mindset beyond individual teams. The entire organizational structure, from leadership down to individual contributors, needs to be aligned with agile principles.

    This alignment requires

    Leadership Buy-In: Agile transformation must start at the top. Leadership teams need to understand and champion agile principles to create an environment where Agile can thrive.

    Structural Adaptation: Organizational structures, roles, and responsibilities may need to be adjusted to accommodate agile practices. This can involve moving away from traditional hierarchies to more flexible, cross-functional teams.

    Continuous Learning: Agile is not a onetime implementation; it's an ongoing journey. Invest in continuous training and coaching to help teams and leaders adapt to agile practices and mindset.

2. Transparency: The Keystone of Agile Success

Transparency is at the heart of agile methodologies. It's not just about visibility into work; it's about creating a culture of openness and collaboration. Transparency ensures that everyone in the organization, from developers to stakeholders, understands the "why" behind agile practices.

This transparency involves

Open and Positive Dialog: Encourage teams to openly discuss challenges and seek solutions collaboratively. Promote positive feedback and constructive criticism to foster a culture of continuous improvement.

Clear Communication: Agile practices like daily stand-ups and sprint reviews are opportunities for clear communication. Ensure that these events focus on meaningful conversations rather than becoming mere rituals.

Visibility into Progress: Use digital tools that provide real-time visibility into project progress. These tools should support agile practices without adding unnecessary complexity.

Agile, in its standard form, often falls short of expectations when not adapted to an organization's unique context. The key to unlocking the true potential of Agile lies in addressing organizational processes and fostering transparency. This may still seem like Agile in many ways, but the reality is that radical transparency and Agile can and do coexist – they just have to adapt to each other and the organization.

Agile is not a destination; it's a journey. It's not just about doing things differently; it's about thinking differently. When organizations embrace agile principles, align their structures, and nurture a culture of transparency and collaboration, they can navigate the agile landscape successfully and reap the rewards of faster delivery, improved quality, and enhanced customer satisfaction.

Let's start to look at how we can transition Agile or move away from its traditional approach into a more radically transparent process that involves your entire organization or at least the key aspects of product and software development within it.

Use Case: Transitioning Away from Agile – The Case of XYZ Corporation

Background

XYZ Corporation, a midsized software development company with a history of agile adoption, found itself at a crossroads. For years, they had faithfully followed agile methodologies, primarily Scrum, believing that it was the ideal approach to managing their software projects. However, as time went on, they began to experience significant challenges that led them to question the effectiveness of Agile in their context.

Challenges Faced

1. Stifled Creativity and Autonomy: Team members at XYZ Corporation began to feel that agile rituals and ceremonies were stifling their creativity and autonomy. Daily stand-up meetings and sprint planning sessions, while designed to enhance collaboration, started feeling like bureaucratic rituals that left little room for individual innovation.

2. Overemphasis on Process: The organization observed that Agile had evolved into a process-heavy framework, with an overemphasis on following predefined practices. The initial promise of adaptability seemed overshadowed by the rigid adherence to Scrum ceremonies.

3. Lack of Clarity: Despite using Agile, XYZ Corporation noticed a lack of clarity regarding project progress and priorities. The Scrum board and burndown charts, meant to provide transparency, often left stakeholders confused about the real status of projects.

4. Team Burnout: Team members were increasingly feeling burnt out due to the pressure of meeting sprint commitments. The relentless pursuit of velocity and sprint goals had begun to negatively impact work–life balance and team morale.

The Decision to Move Away from Agile

In response to these challenges, XYZ Corporation decided to transition away from agile methodologies. They believed that a shift to a more traditional, plan-driven approach would provide the structure and predictability they perceived Agile to lack. Consequently, they began to explore a return to a modified form of the Waterfall model, which they had used in the past.

The Consequences

As XYZ Corporation gradually phased out agile practices, they encountered several issues:

1. Decreased Team Morale: Team morale continued to decline as the rigid structure of the Waterfall model clashed with the autonomy that team members had previously enjoyed in Agile.

2. Communication Breakdown: The absence of daily stand-ups and regular retrospectives led to a breakdown in communication. Team members no longer had a structured forum to discuss project progress and challenges.

3. Loss of Adaptability: While Waterfall provided predictability, it sacrificed adaptability. XYZ Corporation found themselves ill-equipped to respond to changing customer requirements and market dynamics.

4. Increased Project Overheads: The transition to Waterfall reintroduced a significant amount of project management overhead, leading to delays and increased costs.

The Radical Therapy and Radical Transparency Solution

Had XYZ Corporation explored and implemented radical therapy and radical transparency within their agile framework, they might have found a more effective solution to their challenges.

By embracing radical transparency, XYZ Corporation could have enhanced visibility into their projects without abandoning Agile. Daily stand-up meetings and sprint reviews could have been transformed into meaningful dialogues where team members openly discussed challenges and explored solutions. This transparency would have enabled better decision-making and alignment with stakeholders.

It's easy in hindsight to point out these problems and say things like involve stakeholders earlier, create more transparent lines of communication, and bring transparency up to the organizational level, but in practice, it's difficult to do midstream. The goal should be to start to adopt these processes early on, but that's not always the reality. What we want to do is provide ways to identify where the process is going wrong and start to adjust. Here are a few ways we would try to fix this process once it has already started:

1. Encouraging Creativity and Autonomy:

   Challenge: To combat the perception that Agile stifles creativity and autonomy, promote the concept of "innovation time" within the team. Allocate a specific portion of each sprint or week where team members are encouraged to work on individual or small-group innovation projects unrelated to the immediate sprint goals.

   Benefit: This approach allows team members to maintain their autonomy and creative freedom. It also reinforces the idea that Agile is a framework that can be adapted to suit the team's needs.

2. Balancing Process and Adaptability:

   Challenge: To mitigate the overemphasis on processes, consider transitioning from a strict Scrum framework to a more flexible agile approach, such as Kanban. Kanban encourages continuous improvement and doesn't prescribe specific ceremonies. This change can help strike a balance between process and adaptability.

Benefit: Kanban's flexibility allows teams to adapt their workflow to their unique challenges while still following agile principles. It reduces the feeling of rigidity associated with Scrum ceremonies.

3. Enhancing Clarity:

    Challenge: To address the lack of clarity regarding project progress and priorities, create a more comprehensive and visual project dashboard. This dashboard should include not only Scrum artifacts like the Scrum board and burndown charts but also high-level project goals, user stories, and their associated statuses.

    Benefit: A comprehensive dashboard provides stakeholders with a holistic view of the project's status. This increased transparency helps alleviate confusion and provides a clearer understanding of the project's direction.

4. Mitigating Team Burnout:

    Challenge: To combat team burnout, focus on improving work–life balance and setting realistic sprint commitments. Encourage the team to take advantage of the agile principle of "sustainable pace" by revisiting and adjusting sprint goals and velocity expectations.

    Benefit: Prioritizing work–life balance and setting achievable sprint goals can lead to a more motivated and productive team. Reduced burnout contributes to higher morale and better overall project outcomes.

Work–life balance is a polarizing term for many, and for most product teams, especially in startups, it can be incredibly difficult to manage the demands of someone like a founder who does not see a difference between life and work and someone like a remote contractor who feels very little connection to the mission of the product.

A good suggestion might be to replace work–life balance or even home vs. office work with the old adage of me-time. "Me time" can still be on company time; it just needs to be understood why and how it's being taken. You don't need to share or know personal reasons for needing a break during the day or week, but if it's a team problem, it's helpful to share. Remember when 15-minute coffee breaks and 1-hour lunches were part of every office? That's a version of me-time; it just needs to be more flexible than that, and it should be encouraged. Avoiding burnout through time away from your screen or by allowing 10 minutes between meetings doesn't just help your team stay more productive, it also helps your colleagues feel appreciated and part of the organization's long-term plans, not just a resource to be driven until the breaking point.

Real-World Example:

A real-world example that illustrates the potential benefits of radical transparency is the case of Spotify. In 2014, Spotify famously abandoned the traditional model of management, introducing a radical approach known as the "Spotify model." This model emphasized radical transparency through practices like open "guilds" and "chapters" where employees across the organization could openly discuss challenges and collaborate on solutions.

Research Link: [Scaling Agile @ Spotify with Tribes, Squads, Chapters & Guilds] (https://blog.crisp.se/wp-content/uploads/2012/11/SpotifyScaling.pdf)

With radical therapy and some of the suggestions earlier as well as some of the techniques Spotify used, XYZ Corporation could have addressed team burnout and engagement issues. By promoting a culture of positive feedback and open communication, team members would have felt more valued and supported in their roles. This case serves as a valuable lesson that, in the pursuit of project management solutions, it's essential to explore and leverage the full potential of existing methodologies before making a significant shift.

Review

Therapist 1: You know, Therapist 2, I've been reading this fascinating chapter about the agile paradox. It's like a mystery novel, but with software development!

Therapist 2: Oh, do tell! What's this agile paradox all about?

Therapist 1: Well, it's about how organizations often adopt agile methodologies to bring flexibility and creativity to their software projects but sometimes end up drowning in a sea of meetings and processes.

Therapist 2: Ah, the old "too much process, not enough progress" conundrum?

Therapist 1: Exactly! Agile was supposed to be the hero that rescued projects from the clutches of Waterfall, but it seems it brought its own set of challenges. The chapter talks about how teams get caught up in the rituals of Agile – daily stand-ups, sprint planning, retrospectives – to the point where they forget they're actually supposed to be writing code!

Therapist 2: It's like they became agile zombies, obsessed with ceremonies instead of brains!

Therapist 1: (chuckles) Yes, exactly! And they started using pencils, index cards, and sticky notes more than their keyboards!

Therapist 2: Oh, the horror!

Therapist 1: But here's the real kicker – the case study in the chapter is about a company that decided to ditch Agile altogether and go back to Waterfall.

Therapist 2: (gasps) The ultimate plot twist!

Therapist 1: Right? They thought Waterfall would save them from the agile monster. But, as it turns out, they missed the creativity, autonomy, and adaptability they had with Agile.

Therapist 2: So, they went from agile zombies to Waterfall mummies?

Therapist 1: (laughs) It seems that way! And that's where the agile paradox comes in. The chapter suggests that instead of abandoning Agile, they should have embraced radical transparency and radical therapy.

Therapist 2: Radical what now?

Therapist 1: (grinning) Radical transparency – it's like giving your projects a see-through cape! And radical therapy – it's like group counseling for software teams.

Therapist 2: (laughs) So, they could have avoided becoming monsters by being more open and talking about their feelings?

Therapist 1: (nodding) Precisely! They could have had their agility and their process too, without turning into agile zombies or Waterfall mummies.

Therapist 2: Well, isn't that a tale of software development gone wild! I can't wait to read this chapter myself.

Therapist 1: Oh, you'll love it, Therapist 2. It's a real page-turner, full of twists, turns, and sticky notes!

Therapist 2: (laughs) I'm looking forward to it. Thanks for the therapy session, Therapist 1.

Therapist 1: Anytime, Therapist 2. Just remember, when in doubt, add some radical therapy to your agile adventures!

CHAPTER 11

Infinite Possibilities

What Types of Projects Can Use These Methods?

There isn't a limit to the types of projects that can use a more agile or iterative approach to project management. What we are proposing is similar to radical transparency and therapy; it's a way to be more flexible with your project planning and to start building things and getting feedback earlier. The main discomfort will be in exposing your work before it's "done" and finding a way to ensure the feedback you get is constructive.

In software development teams, this is usually done by building an MVP that can be shipped to the end user early as they can provide feedback right away. This also involves beta testing and deploying things that aren't always perfect. That can be uncomfortable, but it helps to involve the end user earlier to ensure you aren't going down the wrong track or that with a few small tweaks or enhancements, you can get back on track if needed.

Each round of changes or enhancements is an iteration and usually results in another deployment to the end user for feedback. The product continues to get better this way and sometimes evolves in a way you never expected because the more people that use it, the more unusual variations they will find for how to use it.

© Gregory Lind, Maryna Mishchenko 2024
G. Lind and M. Mishchenko, *Radical Therapy for Software Development Teams*,
https://doi.org/10.1007/979-8-8688-0187-7_11

Taking that to your personal project or small internal team doesn't mean you lose out on the benefit of being iterative, it just means your feedback is more focused and you have to break your work up into smaller more manageable tasks that can help you get things done faster.

Deadline-Driven Projects with Tight Inflexible Timelines

Take the example of a small advertisement project. Say you want to make and share flyers for an upcoming show. This could be an art show, music or DJ'd concert, or a release party for your new product. Either way you have a list of things you need to remember to get done, and you can't do it all at once. The first thing that probably comes to mind is putting together a list of to-dos and start working from the top.

There is a fairly obvious list of things to do:

- Design flyer.

- Take it to the printer.

- Distribute flyers to businesses.

- Put flyers up on polls and signs.

- Sit back and wait for all the people to show up.

Makes sense, right? For most of us, we wouldn't even need the list. It's all fairly obvious and can get done in less than a day if you rush it. Let's just try and break it up into a few smaller tasks though, involve a couple other people, and see if we can make this a bit better and a bit easier. For fun, let's say we have a week to distribute 1000 of the flyers and have friends/coworkers to help out.

First, let's start with the iterations. There are clearly at least two small iterations and one large iteration here: First, get feedback on your flyer design to make sure everyone agrees with it. Second, split up the distribution of the flyer to each person and have them spread out the coverage across the city in small iterations:

- Design Flyer.

- Get feedback from John and Ringo.

- Revise design.

- Print flyer 500 copies.

- John takes it to business at the waterfront.

- Ringo takes it to signs and polls at the waterfront.

- Print flyer 500 copies.

- John takes it to businesses downtown.

- Ringo takes it to signs and polls downtown.

You could probably add another step by printing fewer flyers at first and getting feedback on the design from the businesses as well, but that depends on the project needs really. Overall, just a couple more steps prepare us for the inevitable feedback and help to distribute the work into iterations so we can get feedback throughout and help improve the end product.

This is bringing an agile-like iterative approach to the design and distribution process while also involving others through transparent feedback. We could improve this of course by getting feedback from customers, or the potential audience, as well as encouraging them to get involved and contribute their own design via a contest with a winner whose design is shared, building a community around your event, and increasing exposure and engagement. You get the idea though that iterative processes along with being transparent and as external as possible can help you build a better product and increase awareness.

Long-Term Maintenance Projects with No End in Sight

Another example might be those ongoing, never-ending but still just as important to the bottom-line maintenance projects. We more than likely already do these iterations. We plan out a list of tasks for the week or the month that need to get done, assign them, and share our progress the next week. Maybe you use a planning meeting or software to manage the progress and communication, but it's still an iterative process. We can document that in the same way with milestones, weekly sprints, daily stand-ups, and even estimates and progress for each iteration.

The process is still the same, but in the end, we are following a more flexible process that could have any number of variations – customer demands for changes, supply levels that need to be managed, or new team members that need to be onboarded. Documenting this process and sharing the optimizations or changes you make can be the difference in success or failure for tasks for the week or the month that need to get done, assign them, and share our progress the next week. Maybe you use a planning meeting or software to manage the progress and communication, but it's still an iterative process. We can document that in the same way with milestones, weekly sprints, daily stand-ups, and even estimates and progress for each iteration.

Customer demands for changes, supply levels that need to be managed, or new team members that need to be onboarded all of these can now be handled more transparently and iteratively allowing to break down tasks and plan accordingly. Documenting this process and sharing the optimizations or changes you make can be the difference in success or failure for your project. When others share their approaches or you find a template that illustrates the obvious step you have been missing all this time, you not only increase the viability of the product, but you improve your process for next time.

Sustaining Progress Through the Product Life Cycle Journey

Especially within the agile framework, competitive advantage is the cornerstone of success. It's not just about writing code or managing projects; it's about crafting products that not only satisfy user needs but also set you apart from the competition. When you work on real-world products with physical components like building a house or manufacturing a car, it can seem like agile and software-based approaches are impossible. The reality is that when you take Agile and radical transparency, you can improve product processes like design, construction, and customer feedback to the point it starts to feel like you are working with virtual blocks before they have been placed and getting feedback earlier to avoid long-term problems.

Early Warning System

Early Warning System: The Guardian of Product Success in Agile Development

Agile principles aren't limited to software; they can enhance the development of real-world physical products as well. Just as in software, establishing an early warning system is paramount to ensure the success of your physical product. Here's how you can set up an effective early warning system for any real-world product, integrating the concept of radical transparency:

Monitoring for Bugs and Issues:

Robust monitoring and testing tools are your initial defense in agile development for physical products. Implement continuous quality checks, automated testing, and performance evaluations to scrutinize your product's performance. Embrace the iterative approach of Agile, which entails continuous building and testing, ensuring that issues are detected early and addressed transparently.

Frequent and Structured Feedback:

Product development thrives on feedback, and this remains true for physical products. In an agile context, actively seek feedback at every stage of development, emphasizing transparency:

Development Team and Stakeholder Feedback:

Regularly solicit input from your development team, product managers, and stakeholders. Integrate feedback loops into your development process, aligning them with project milestones and crucial decision points.

User Feedback:

End users remain pivotal in providing insights into your product's usability and functionality. Engage users in the feedback process:

- User Testing and Prototyping: Conduct user testing sessions and prototype evaluations, involving users in assessing the product's physical attributes. Analyze user feedback meticulously, categorizing issues transparently by severity and priority. In the spirit of Agile, integrate user feedback into future development cycles promptly.

The Product Manager's Role in Transparency:

Product managers continue to play a central role in agile development for physical products. They serve as the voice of the customer within the team, ensuring that user needs are met. To enhance transparency

- Direct Communication: Product managers should maintain open lines of communication with developers, actively seeking feedback from both the team and users. Translate this feedback into actionable insights and tasks, sharing this process transparently with the team.

Regular Inspection and Adaptation:

Implement the concept of "inspection and adaptation" proactively:

- Regular Product Evaluation: Organize regular product evaluations within your development team. These sessions encourage a critical examination of the physical product, uncovering issues that may not be apparent during routine work. Transparency is crucial in documenting and addressing these discoveries.

Frequent Feedback Cycles: Where and When?

Incorporate transparency into the rhythm of your project:

- Daily Stand-Ups: Like in software, daily stand-up meetings provide an excellent forum for exchanging feedback. Encourage open discussions about potential issues or roadblocks, fostering a transparent environment.

- User Testing Sessions: Continue to encourage user testing and feedback at various stages of physical product development, holding sessions after each development cycle to ensure transparency in addressing user concerns.

- Beta Testing: Embrace beta testing to align with Agile's iterative nature. Engage a select group of users in beta testing, enabling rapid iteration and issue resolution before a wider release.

- Feedback Forms: Integrate feedback mechanisms within the product, allowing users to provide insights easily. Regularly analyze this feedback transparently to identify recurring issues.

- Regular Retrospectives: After each development cycle, schedule retrospectives where the team reflects on successes, challenges, and process improvements. Transparency is key to resolving identified issues promptly.

Balancing User and Product Manager Feedback:

In Agile, where user-centricity is paramount, it's essential to strike a balance between user feedback and product manager input, aligning them with the product's vision and strategy. Product managers play a crucial role in this balancing act, collaborating transparently:

- User Feedback Alignment: Product managers should consider user feedback while transparently aligning it with the product's long-term goals, ensuring that the team and users remain on the same page.

In agile development, competitive advantage stems not only from innovation but also from adaptability and the ability to learn from feedback swiftly. Establishing an early warning system, consistently seeking feedback, and managing it transparently are pivotal steps in maintaining your competitive edge within the agile framework, whether applied to software or real-world physical products.

Review

Therapist 1: Well, my friend, we've reached Chapter 11, and it's all about "Infinite Possibilities" in project management. You know, I'm starting to think the authors might be optimists.

Therapist 2: You might be onto something. But hey, infinite possibilities, that's exciting, right?

Therapist 1: Absolutely! The author insists that there are no limits to the types of projects that can use agile or iterative approaches combined with radical transparency.

Therapist 2: Oh, that's where I have a bone to pick. I mean, not every project can be all warm and fuzzy with iterative methods. What about those strict, deadline-driven projects?

Therapist 1: You're right, the authors do mention those. Imagine trying to organize a flyer distribution for an event. Seems straightforward, right?

Therapist 2: Yeah, I mean, design the flyer, print it, distribute it, done!

Therapist 1: But hold on a minute! These authors suggest breaking it down into iterations. Design the flyer, get feedback, revise, print half, distribute to one area, and then repeat.

Therapist 2: That sounds like an awful lot of work for something as simple as flyers.

Therapist 1: I know, right? But the point is to involve others, get feedback, and make it better. It's like a flyer revolution!

Therapist 2: Well, okay, I guess there's something to be said about involving people and getting feedback. But what about never-ending maintenance projects?

Therapist 1: Ah, you mean those projects that just seem to go on forever?

Therapist 2: Exactly! How can you apply this iterative stuff to that?

Therapist 1: The authors insist that it's possible. You just need to be flexible, document your progress, and share it transparently.

Therapist 2: I see what they're getting at, but in the real world, things can get messy. Customer demands change, new team members join, and you're telling me all of this can be handled transparently and iteratively?

Therapist 1: That's the idea! It's about adapting and learning from feedback.

Therapist 2: Well, I suppose there's something to be said about staying flexible and open to change. But what really got me is when they talked about applying all this to building physical products, like houses or cars.

Therapist 1: I know, it seems a bit far-fetched, doesn't it? But the author argues that with radical transparency, you can improve design, construction, and even customer feedback.

Therapist 2: It's like working with virtual blocks before they're even placed!

Therapist 1: Exactly! So, even in the world of bricks and mortar, there's room for a little agile magic.

Therapist 2: Well, I may not agree with everything they say, but I can't deny that there are some intriguing possibilities here.

Therapist 1: Agreed, even if we don't buy into all of it, there's no harm in exploring these infinite possibilities, right?

Therapist 2: Absolutely. Who knows, we might stumble upon a few golden nuggets of wisdom along the way.

CHAPTER 12

Radical Therapy for Your Organization

Implementing a policy of radical transparency and positive reinforcement for your project or product is a great starting point. In the end though, you have to get organizational "buy-in" to make it succeed, and in order for an organization to enact such a policy, they likely and probably should want to enact it at every level.

Depending on the size and age of the organization you work in, getting buy-in for transparency alone can seem like an impossible task. Let's go through some steps we can take to get started, some small, some bigger, to help your organization get started where they can and illustrate the areas where it's needed, if not essential.

Guide to Achieving Organizational Buy-In for Radical Transparency and Positive Reinforcement

Gaining organizational buy-in for radical transparency and positive reinforcement is essential to foster a culture of innovation, collaboration, and productivity. In this guide, we provide an in-depth approach to securing support at all levels of the organization, along with strategies

G. Lind and M. Mishchenko, *Radical Therapy for Software Development Teams*, https://doi.org/10.1007/979-8-8688-0187-7_12

for transparent reporting that highlight benefits, align with stakeholder interests, and address critical issues like climate change.

Embrace Transparent Communication

Radical transparency starts with open communication. Demonstrate how clear communication promotes shared understanding and reduces misunderstandings. Reference studies like a *Harvard Business Review* article that states, "Transparent organizations are 20% more likely to report higher levels of trust among employees." Transparency fosters a culture where team members feel valued and informed, enhancing collaboration and productivity:

1. Lead by Example: Leaders and managers should set the tone for transparent communication. They should openly share information, be approachable, and encourage open dialogue.

2. Use Clear and Accessible Channels: Ensure that communication channels are clear and accessible to all team members. This includes using tools like email, team messaging apps, or project management software to share information and updates.

3. Regular Updates: Provide regular updates on project progress, company performance, and any changes in strategy. This helps team members stay informed about what's happening.

4. Encourage Questions: Create an environment where team members feel comfortable asking questions and seeking clarification. This can be done through regular Q&A sessions or open-door policies.

5. Share Goals and Objectives: Make sure everyone understands the organization's goals and objectives. When team members know what they are working toward, they are more likely to align their efforts.

6. Feedback Mechanisms: Implement feedback mechanisms that allow team members to provide input on decisions, processes, and improvements. Act on this feedback when possible, demonstrating that it's valued.

7. Transparency in Decision-Making: Be transparent about how decisions are made. This includes sharing the reasoning behind choices, even if they are unpopular.

8. Training and Education: Provide training and resources on effective communication and transparency. This can help team members develop the skills needed for open and honest communication.

9. Celebrate Successes and Learn from Failures: Recognize and celebrate achievements and milestones. Similarly, when things don't go as planned, openly discuss what went wrong and how to improve.

10. Document Policies and Procedures: Have clear documentation of company policies and procedures. This ensures that everyone has access to the same information and reduces misunderstandings.

11. Privacy and Sensitivity: While transparency is essential, be mindful of sensitive information. Not everything can or should be shared openly. Clearly define what can and cannot be disclosed.

12. Consistency: Maintain consistency in communication. Regularly scheduled updates and meetings can help establish a routine for open communication.

Remember that achieving radical transparency especially the important aspect of communication might require a cultural shift within an organization, and it may not happen overnight. It's an ongoing process that requires commitment from leadership and active participation from all team members.

Link Transparency to Productivity

Illustrate how transparent reporting enhances productivity. Cite real-world examples of organizations that saw increased efficiency after implementing transparency measures. A *Forbes* study showed that teams with transparent communication practices are 50% more likely to meet project deadlines. Transparent reporting enables swift decision-making and proactive problem-solving, minimizing delays.

Link Transparency to Productivity:

Improved Accountability: Transparent reporting creates a sense of accountability among team members. When everyone can see the progress and performance metrics, individuals are more likely to take ownership of their tasks and deadlines.

Reduced Miscommunication: Transparency minimizes misunderstandings and miscommunication. When information is readily available, team members are less likely to waste time seeking clarification or resolving conflicts arising from incomplete or inaccurate data.

Enhanced Collaboration: Open access to project status and data fosters collaboration. Team members can better align their efforts when they have visibility into each other's work, leading to more efficient problem-solving and resource allocation.

Swift Decision-Making: Transparency enables faster decision-making. When relevant data is easily accessible, leaders and teams can make informed decisions promptly, preventing bottlenecks and project delays.

Proactive Problem-Solving: With transparent reporting, issues and roadblocks are identified earlier in the process. Teams can proactively address these challenges, preventing them from escalating into major setbacks that can impact productivity.

Examples of Organizations Benefiting from Transparency Measures:

> Google: Google is known for its culture of transparency, where employees have access to a wealth of information, including company financials and product development updates. This transparency encourages employees to contribute ideas, collaborate across departments, and take ownership of projects, ultimately driving productivity.

> Buffer: Buffer, a social media management platform, practices radical transparency by sharing employee salaries, equity details, and even emails from the CEO to the entire team. This transparency has built trust within the organization, leading to improved focus on work and increased productivity.

> Zappos: The online shoe and clothing retailer Zappos is famous for its transparent organizational structure and the use of Holacracy, a self-management system. This approach empowers

employees to make decisions autonomously and participate in transparent governance, resulting in a more productive and agile organization.

W. L. Gore & Associates: This global materials science company operates with a flat organizational structure and practices transparency by openly sharing financial information with all associates. This approach has led to high levels of trust and engagement, driving innovation and productivity.

Atlassian: The software company Atlassian practices transparency by sharing product road maps, company values, and financial results with employees. This transparency helps employees understand the company's goals and their role in achieving them, leading to increased productivity.

Demonstrate Impact with Data

Use data-driven insights to showcase the impact of radical transparency on project outcomes. Share metrics that demonstrate improved collaboration, reduced conflicts, and accelerated decision-making. *Forbes* highlighted a company that increased its revenue by 10% after implementing transparent reporting, demonstrating the tangible benefits of this approach.

Demonstrate Impact with Data:

Define Key Metrics: Begin by defining key performance metrics that are relevant to your organization's goals and projects. These metrics could include project completion times, team collaboration scores, conflict resolution times, or any other indicators of project success.

Baseline Measurement: Before implementing radical transparency, measure and establish a baseline for these metrics. This will serve as a point of comparison for post-transparency data.

Implement Transparency: Introduce radical transparency practices, such as open access to project data, clear communication channels, and shared decision-making processes. Ensure that everyone understands the new transparency measures and is actively participating.

Collect Data: Continuously collect data related to the defined metrics during and after the implementation of transparency. This data can be gathered through project management tools, surveys, feedback sessions, and performance evaluations.

Analyze Results: Use data analysis techniques to assess the impact of transparency. Compare post-transparency data to the baseline measurements. Look for trends, patterns, and statistically significant changes in the chosen metrics.

Highlight Improvements: Showcase the positive changes brought about by radical transparency. Use visualizations, charts, and reports to make the data easily understandable. Emphasize improvements in collaboration, conflict resolution, decision-making speed, and any other relevant areas.

Examples of Impact with Data:

Faster Decision-Making: Measure the average time it takes to make critical project decisions before and after implementing transparency. If the time to decision decreases significantly, it demonstrates the positive impact of transparency on decision-making speed.

Reduced Conflict Resolution Time: Track how long it takes to resolve conflicts or issues within projects. If this time is reduced after implementing transparency, it indicates that open communication is helping teams address challenges more efficiently.

Improved Collaboration Scores: Use surveys or collaboration assessment tools to measure team collaboration and satisfaction levels.

If scores increase after embracing transparency, it suggests that teams are working better together.

Project Completion Times: Measure how quickly projects are completed, comparing projects managed with and without radical transparency. If projects are consistently finished faster, it illustrates the efficiency gains from transparency.

Revenue Growth: If applicable, measure the impact on revenue or profitability. Highlight any revenue growth or cost savings achieved after implementing transparency, as *Forbes* mentioned in its case study.

Employee Satisfaction: Survey employees about their satisfaction with the new transparent practices. Increased employee satisfaction can correlate with improved project outcomes.

By using data to demonstrate the impact of radical transparency, organizations can provide concrete evidence of its benefits. This approach helps stakeholders understand how transparency positively affects project outcomes, leading to improved decision-making, collaboration, and overall success.

Build Trust Through Transparency

Highlight how transparency builds trust among stakeholders, including investors, grantors, and customers. Cite the Edelman Trust Barometer, which found that transparent companies are perceived as more trustworthy by 73% of surveyed consumers. Transparent reporting reassures stakeholders that the organization is committed to ethical practices and accountability:

Investors: Transparency is a cornerstone of investor relations. When investors have access to clear, accurate, and timely information about a company's financial health, operations, and decision-making processes, it instills confidence. Investors are more likely to support organizations that openly communicate their plans, challenges, and successes.

Grantors: Organizations seeking grants or funding from foundations, government agencies, or philanthropic entities benefit from transparency. Grantors want to ensure that their funds are used effectively and in alignment with their mission. Transparent reporting assures grantors that their investments are well-managed and achieving the intended impact.

Customers: Transparency is a powerful tool for customer trust and loyalty. When companies openly share information about their products, services, pricing, and ethical practices, it creates a sense of authenticity. Customers are more likely to choose businesses they trust, and transparent organizations are perceived as more honest and accountable.

Accountability: Transparency demonstrates a commitment to accountability. When organizations openly report on their actions and outcomes, they signal that they are willing to take responsibility for their decisions, both positive and negative. This accountability fosters trust among stakeholders who appreciate the willingness to learn from mistakes and make improvements.

Ethical Practices: Transparent reporting reinforces an organization's commitment to ethical practices. It shows that the company has nothing to hide and is willing to subject itself to scrutiny. This commitment to ethics reassures stakeholders that the organization operates with integrity.

Long-Term Benefits: Building trust through transparency is not just about short-term gains. It establishes a foundation for long-term, sustainable relationships with stakeholders. Organizations that consistently demonstrate transparency are more likely to retain investor support, secure grants, and maintain customer loyalty over time.

Shift from Proprietary to Collaborative Culture

Discuss how the traditional culture of proprietary information contributes to distrust and stifles innovation. Emphasize that the shift to transparency aligns with the global movement toward ethical and sustainable business practices.

For decades, many organizations operated under a culture of hoarding information as a means of maintaining a competitive edge. Proprietary information was closely guarded, often accessible only to select individuals or departments. While this approach may have been effective in the past, it has significant drawbacks in today's rapidly evolving business landscape.

The hoarding of information fosters an environment of secrecy, which inevitably leads to distrust. When employees feel that information is being withheld, they become suspicious of the organization's motives. This lack of trust can erode morale, hinder collaboration, and even drive talented individuals away from the company.

Proprietary information cultures tend to prioritize protecting existing knowledge over fostering innovation. When information is compartmentalized, employees may lack the insights and data necessary to generate creative ideas or solutions. Innovation thrives on open communication and the free flow of information.

There is plenty of existing research that supports the fact that employees believe a transparent culture leads to better teamwork and collaboration, underscoring the transformative impact of transparency. Openness and honesty create a sense of inclusion, where employees feel valued and informed. When employees trust that information is accessible and shared fairly, they are more likely to collaborate effectively.

The shift toward transparency is not isolated; it aligns with the broader global movement toward ethical and sustainable business practices. Modern consumers and stakeholders are increasingly concerned about how organizations operate. They seek transparency in areas like environmental practices, labor conditions, and supply chain ethics. Companies that embrace transparency demonstrate their commitment to ethical behavior and sustainability, meeting the expectations of an informed and conscientious market.

In today's competitive landscape, innovation is a key driver of success. Organizations that can adapt quickly, respond to changing market dynamics, and generate fresh ideas gain a significant competitive advantage. Transparency promotes innovation by ensuring that employees have access to the information and insights needed to identify opportunities and challenges.

Shifting away from a culture of proprietary information toward one of transparency is not just a trend; it's a strategic imperative. It fosters trust among employees, customers, investors, and other stakeholders. It also unlocks the potential for innovation by democratizing access to information. Ultimately, organizations that embrace transparency position themselves as ethical, sustainable, and innovative leaders in their respective industries.

Engage Leadership on Climate Transparency

If you don't think software and software development processes can help with the battle for climate change, well, just ask some developers what they are doing around greening data centers or improving web conferencing and communication tools to help reduce trips to the office.

Showcase how transparent reporting on climate initiatives can align with executive leadership's commitment to corporate social responsibility. Highlight companies that faced reputational damage due to lack of climate transparency. Cite research on how transparent climate reporting enhances investor confidence and long-term value.

Create a Transparent Reporting Framework

Recommend a transparent reporting framework that spans from project teams to the executive suite. Advocate for regular reporting that showcases progress, setbacks, and lessons learned. Use specific examples to illustrate how transparency not only facilitates communication but also drives continuous improvement and innovation.

Project Team Level:

Daily Stand-Up Meetings: Project teams should conduct daily stand-up meetings where team members provide brief updates on their progress, challenges, and goals for the day. This practice enhances real-time communication and identifies roadblocks early.

Weekly Sprint Reviews: At the end of each week or sprint, project teams should hold review meetings. During these sessions, they showcase what they've accomplished, what didn't go as planned, and what they've learned. The focus should be on transparency and candid discussions.

Department or Division Level:

Biweekly or Monthly Progress Reports: Departments or divisions should compile and share biweekly or monthly progress reports. These reports should include a summary of individual project updates, key performance metrics, and a section on lessons learned. The reports should be accessible to all team members within the department.

Quarterly Review Meetings: Hold quarterly review meetings that involve all teams within a department or division. Share the progress reports, highlight notable achievements, and discuss areas for improvement transparently.

Executive Suite Level:

Monthly Executive Summaries: The executive team should receive monthly executive summaries that consolidate key highlights and challenges from each department or division. These summaries should also include aggregated performance metrics and an emphasis on lessons learned. The review and feedback on these should also be reported back to the teams that submitted them, as well as much detail as possible around new initiatives that are discussed at the executive level.

Quarterly Strategy Reviews: Conduct quarterly strategy reviews at the executive level. These sessions should include deep dives into departmental reports, discussions on cross-functional initiatives, and a focus on aligning strategies with lessons learned and innovation opportunities. Share them internally with teams and externally with advisors, investors, and even customers where you can.

Emphasize that this framework promotes a culture of continuous improvement. By regularly sharing setbacks and lessons learned, teams can collectively identify areas for enhancement and innovation.

Provide examples of how transparency in reporting can lead to innovation. For instance, when teams openly discuss failures or challenges, it often sparks creative problem-solving and the development of new approaches.

Highlight how transparent reporting provides data for informed decision-making. Leaders can make more strategic choices when they have access to real-time project data and insights into what works and what doesn't. Stress the importance of alignment across the organization. When teams and departments openly share their progress, it becomes easier to identify synergies, share best practices, and collaborate on cross-functional projects.

Transparency in reporting fosters employee engagement. Team members feel more valued when their contributions, successes, and challenges are acknowledged and discussed openly. Point out that early identification of setbacks and risks through transparent reporting allows for proactive risk mitigation strategies. This can prevent minor issues from escalating into major problems.

Securing organizational buy-in for radical transparency and positive reinforcement requires a comprehensive approach that emphasizes the benefits of open communication, links transparency to productivity and trust, addresses critical issues like climate change, and advocates for a cultural shift from proprietary practices. Organizations that cultivate a transparent culture not only improve teamwork and creativity but also adhere to morally and environmentally responsible business practices.

Sources:

1. Grant, A. M., & Mayer, D. M. (2009). Good soldiers and good actors: Prosocial and impression management motives as interactive predictors of affiliative citizenship behaviors. *Journal of Applied Psychology*, 94(4), 900-912. (https://psycnet.apa. org/record/2009-10167-015)

2. Edelman Trust Barometer. (2021). www.edelman.com/sites/g/files/aatuss191/ files/2021-01/2021-edelman-trust- barometer.pdf

3. *Forbes*. (2021). Nine Ways To Maintain Clear, Transparent Communication At Your Growing Company www.forbes.com/sites/theyec/2021/08/24/ nine-ways-to-maintain-clear-transparent- communication-at-your-growing-company/

4. McKinsey & Company. (2020). Climate risks and response. www.mckinsey.com/~/media/McKinsey/ Business%20Functions/Sustainability/Our%20 Insights/Climate%20risk%20and%20response%20 Physical%20hazards%20and%20socioeconomic%20 impacts/MGI-Climate-risk-and-response- Executive-summary-vF.pdf

5. Global Reporting Initiative (GRI). (2020). Sustainability and Transparency: A Guide to GRI 306: Efforts to Address Climate Change. www.globalreporting.org/standards/ media/2573/gri-306-waste-2020.pdf

Lack of Transparency and Its Consequences

Transparency is a cornerstone of ethical business practices, yet many large organizations have faced serious repercussions due to a lack of transparency. This lack has not only undermined their credibility but has also resulted in severe legal, political, and reputational fallout. One striking example of this pertains to the issue of climate change, where organizations failing to disclose environmental impacts have faced substantial consequences.

One of the most notable instances of a lack of transparency is the concealment of environmental impact data related to climate change. Organizations that downplayed or concealed their contributions to climate change have encountered harsh consequences. The Volkswagen (VW) emissions scandal is a glaring illustration. In 2015, VW admitted to equipping diesel cars with software that manipulated emissions test results. The deception resulted in fines, lawsuits, and a significant dent in the company's reputation. The incident underscored the potential legal and financial ramifications of not being forthright about environmental practices (www.nber.org/system/files/working_papers/w26117/w26117.pdf).

The lack of transparency regarding corporate practices has often led to legal and political backlash. The ExxonMobil case is a stark example. Investigative reports revealed that Exxon had knowledge of the climate impact of its products for decades but deliberately downplayed this information. This lack of transparency sparked lawsuits and investigations by attorneys general, accusing the company of deceiving investors and the public. Such instances demonstrate the legal jeopardy and public outcry that can ensue when organizations prioritize secrecy over accountability (source: www.theguardian.com/environment/2022/may/24/exxon-trial-climate-crimes-fossil-fuels-global-heating).

Organizations that engage in cover-ups erode stakeholder trust and damage their reputation. BP's Deepwater Horizon oil spill is a pertinent example. The company's lack of transparency about safety and environmental risks not only led to the largest marine oil spill in history but also incurred severe reputational damage and a steep decline in stock value. The incident highlighted how a lack of transparency can undermine public trust, resulting in long-lasting repercussions (source: `www.epa.gov/enforcement/deepwater-horizon-bp-gulf-mexico-oil-spill#:~:text=On%20April%2020%2C%202010%2C%20the,of%20marine%20oil%20drilling%20operations`).

The lack of transparency within large organizations, particularly in the context of climate change cover-ups, has consistently proven to be detrimental. From legal and political consequences to reputational damage and stakeholder mistrust, organizations that prioritize secrecy over accountability often face severe fallout. These cases serve as cautionary tales, emphasizing the critical need for organizations to embrace radical transparency not only for ethical reasons but also as a strategic approach to maintaining credibility, fostering trust, and navigating complex challenges.

Review

Therapist 1: Have you ever heard of radical transparency in organizations?

Therapist 2: Oh yes, it's like a corporate colonoscopy, isn't it? Clears the mind and the... urrr.

Therapist 1: You could say that. It's all about being open, honest, and accountable in the business world. And I've just read a chapter that dives deep into it.

Therapist 2: Interesting! Tell me more.

Therapist 1: Well, this chapter is like the therapist for organizations. It helps them understand the importance of transparency and positive reinforcement.

Therapist 2: Positive reinforcement, you say?

Therapist 1: Yes! Like giving organizations a pat on the back when they're good and helping them improve when they're not.

Therapist 2: (laughs) That's a unique approach!

Therapist 1: Absolutely! And it's all about getting everyone on board, from the top brass to the interns.

Therapist 2: So, how do they start this therapy session?

Therapist 1: First, they embrace transparent communication. No more corporate secrets or hiding the truth.

Therapist 2: (nodding) Like a group therapy session where everyone shares their feelings?

Therapist 1: Exactly! It builds trust and makes everyone feel valued, just like in group therapy. And you know what the chapter says? Transparent organizations are 20% more likely to report higher levels of trust among employees.

Therapist 2: That's quite a statistic!

Therapist 1: And it doesn't stop there. They also link transparency to productivity. When everyone knows what's going on, projects run smoother. Forbes *even says that teams with transparent communication practices are 50% more likely to meet project deadlines.*

Therapist 2: Wow, that's some serious progress!

Therapist 1: And here's the best part – they use data to demonstrate the impact. Metrics, metrics, metrics! Like how one company increased its revenue by 10% after being transparent.

Therapist 2: So, it's not just talk, but it's backed by results!

Therapist 1: Precisely! And they also build trust through transparency, which is like rebuilding trust in a broken relationship.

Therapist 2: And what's this about climate transparency?

Therapist 1: Ah, that's a special session! Organizations showcase their efforts to combat climate change. It's like environmental therapy for them.

Therapist 2: (laughs) So, this chapter is like a comprehensive therapy plan for organizations.

Therapist 1: Absolutely! It's about nurturing transparency and positive reinforcement. Because, you see, if you don't deal with your issues, you end up like those organizations that faced legal trouble, political backlash, and reputational damage.

Therapist 2: (smiles) So, radical transparency is like corporate therapy, but it's also a smart business move?

Therapist 1: You got it! It's therapy with a return on investment.

Therapist 2: (laughs) Well, I'm convinced. I think every organization could use a bit of this therapy!

Therapist 1: I couldn't agree more, Therapist 2. It's time for some corporate healing!

CHAPTER 13

Fostering Empathy and Resilience

Understanding Burnout in Software Development

In software development and product management, where innovation and productivity reign supreme, the shadow of burnout can loom large and persist. The relentless pursuit of excellence, unwavering project demands, and the ceaseless pressure to deliver can leave a lasting mark on even the most passionate and dedicated teams. But burnout is not an inevitable fate; it's a challenge that can be met with empathy, resilience, and a commitment to change. Burnout is more than just exhaustion; it's a pervasive sense of physical and emotional depletion that can affect individuals and teams alike. In the context of radical therapy for software development, where open communication and empathy are central, burnout can manifest in various forms. It affects productivity, stifles creativity, and can bring feelings of despair and detachment from the work at hand.

© Gregory Lind, Maryna Mishchenko 2024
G. Lind and M. Mishchenko, *Radical Therapy for Software Development Teams*,
https://doi.org/10.1007/979-8-8688-0187-7_13

Recognizing Burnout

Recognizing the early signs of burnout is important for fostering a healthy and resilient team. While the overt indicators may include waning motivation, increased absenteeism, and a decline in the quality of work, a more nuanced understanding is essential. Here we will delve into a comprehensive approach to recognizing burnout, drawing from both anecdotal evidence and empirical research.

Observable Signs

- Waning Motivation: Keep a keen eye on team members exhibiting a noticeable decrease in enthusiasm and motivation. A sudden lack of interest in work that was once approached with vigor may indicate burnout.

- Increased Absenteeism: Frequent and unexplained absences can be a red flag. While everyone has occasional off-days, a pattern of absenteeism may signal deeper underlying issues.

Quality of Work

- Decline in Work Quality: The manifestation of burnout often reflects in the output. Look for a notable drop in the quality of work, missed deadlines, or an increase in errors. These are tangible signs that the team member may be grappling with burnout.

Behavioral Changes

- Frequent Frustration: Burnout can lead to heightened frustration, often expressed through increased irritability or impatience. Team members who were once patient and composed may exhibit a notable shift in demeanor.

- Persistent Fatigue: Chronic exhaustion, both physical and mental, is a common hallmark of burnout. If team members consistently appear fatigued, even after breaks, it warrants attention.

Emotional Indicators

- Disengagement: Apathy and disengagement from team activities or discussions can be indicative of burnout. Team members may withdraw from collaborative efforts, signaling a need for intervention.

Research and Studies

Maslach Burnout Inventory (MBI)

The Maslach Burnout Inventory is a widely used tool for assessing burnout. It categorizes burnout into three components: emotional exhaustion, depersonalization, and reduced personal accomplishment. Regularly employing such validated assessments can provide a quantifiable measure of burnout levels within a team. Maslach-Burnout-Inventory-MBI.pdf (different.hr)

The Influence of Leadership Styles

Research by McKinsey & Company suggests that leadership styles play a pivotal role in preventing burnout. Leaders who prioritize transparent communication and foster a positive work environment contribute significantly to mitigating burnout risks. What is burnout? | McKinsey

Recognizing burnout demands a multifaceted approach, combining observable signs, behavioral changes, and emotional indicators. Drawing insights from empirical research provides a solid foundation for understanding the intricacies of burnout within the unique context of software development and product management teams.

Nurturing Empathy

Empathy serves as the bedrock of addressing burnout effectively, especially within the radical therapy approach. As a manager or team leader, it's essential to understand and genuinely care about your team's challenges, frustrations, and emotional well-being. Acknowledge their efforts, and express authentic concern for their welfare. In the context of radical therapy, empathy isn't just about understanding; it's about showing that you genuinely care.

Fostering Open Communication and Creating Psychological Safety

Within the radical therapy paradigm, psychological safety takes center stage. It's about fostering an atmosphere where team members feel secure in expressing their thoughts without fear of judgment or repercussions. By removing the stigma associated with vulnerability, you empower individuals to bring their authentic selves to the professional forefront.

Research, notably by Harvard Business School professor Amy Edmondson (2018), has emphasized the concept of psychological safety in teams. Within the radical therapy paradigm, fostering psychological safety allows team members to express their thoughts and feelings without fear of judgment or reprisal. This not only enhances the overall team dynamic but also acts as a vital component in preventing and addressing burnout www.hbs.edu/faculty/Pages/item.aspx?num=54851). Open and honest communication is not a onetime event; it's a continuous dialogue that evolves. Encourage team members to articulate their struggles, concerns, and sources of stress without reservation. This might involve regular check-ins, team meetings designed for sharing, or even anonymous feedback channels. The goal is to create a culture where transparency is the norm, not the exception.

In the radical therapy approach, every voice is a valuable instrument in the orchestra of collaboration. Team members need to know that their voices are not only heard but genuinely valued. Recognition and acknowledgment of their perspectives, experiences, and ideas contribute to a sense of belonging and significance within the team. This validation builds trust and fosters a collective responsibility for each other's well-being.

Open dialogue serves as a powerful tool for understanding the nuances of burnout within the team. Team members sharing their experiences can offer valuable insights into the root causes of burnout. This information is instrumental in identifying patterns, triggers, and areas that require intervention. It transforms the team into active participants in the burnout prevention process.

Fostering open communication is not just about identifying problems; it's about collaboratively working on solutions. In the radical therapy framework, the team becomes a collective force, brainstorming strategies to alleviate stressors, improve work processes, and enhance overall well-being. In addition to addressing burnout, this cooperative approach to problem-solving builds the team's resilience.

Flexible Work Arrangements

Software development is notorious for its unpredictable workloads and the occasional sprint toward project deadlines. Recognizing this, the radical therapy paradigm acknowledges the need for a flexible approach that adapts to the dynamic nature of the industry. It's not about compromising productivity; it's about enhancing it through a more balanced and sustainable work environment. Allowing team members the flexibility to work from different locations fosters autonomy and reduces the stress associated with commuting. This approach acknowledges the diverse needs of the team, catering to individuals who may thrive in nontraditional work settings. Another aspect is flexibility in work hours. It is a key element within the radical therapy paradigm. Acknowledging that not everyone operates at their peak during traditional 9-to-5 hours, this approach empowers individuals to tailor their workday to their unique circadian rhythms. Whether it's starting later in the morning or working into the evening, flexible hours ensure that team members can optimize their productivity without compromising their well-being.

Compressed workweeks, another facet of the radical therapy approach, involve condensing the standard five-day workweek into fewer days. For example, team members might work four longer days instead of five regular ones. This arrangement provides extended periods for rest and rejuvenation, promoting a healthier work–life balance.

Empowering Work–Life Harmony

The emphasis on flexible work arrangements within the radical therapy paradigm is rooted in the belief that a harmonious integration of work and life is achievable. It's not about working less but about working smarter and creating an environment where individuals can thrive both professionally and personally. By offering options that align with individual preferences, the paradigm recognizes and addresses the diverse needs of the team. The ultimate goal of flexible work arrangements is to reduce stress and enhance overall well-being. It's an acknowledgment that a one-size-fits-all approach to work may not be the most effective or sustainable. By providing choices that cater to the individual, the paradigm aims to create a workplace where burnout is not just mitigated but replaced by a culture of empowerment and fulfillment.

Promoting Work–Life Balance

The radical therapy paradigm champions the notion that taking regular breaks is not a sign of idleness but a strategic move to enhance overall productivity. By encouraging team members to step away from their tasks periodically, the paradigm aims to refresh their minds, preventing burnout and promoting sustained focus.

Here comes that term again though, work–life balance? It's not the same for everyone, and for many, they don't agree there should be a difference between work–life and life. It's just balance. Well, that's not so bad though right? Balance, like we talked about before with the idea of me-time wherever you are – me-time at work, me-time at home. If you are working remotely, there is little difference, but maybe you are there to be. Regardless of what you call it, you, your team, and your organization need to be on the same page about the need for this type of balance and how and when can you take that time to get the things done you need outside of your issue backlog, or product meetings, or the typical work you do.

Education and training are part of that as well; we all want to learn and better ourselves, and sometimes the organization we work for helps with that. Should there be a reward for that or is it that you getting better at your job is the reward? Or maybe you should be taking on the initiative to make yourself better and that should be part of your me-time? It's not easy, and everyone has a different opinion on it as well as different circumstances. Maybe you have a family at home that needs more of your time now than they did. Or maybe you have a partner or significant other who is sick and needs you to take care of them more. It all falls under time you need to take away from what you might regularly be doing, and you and your organization need to have a plan for how to handle that. An organization that doesn't have a strategy and refuses to put one in place may have its values and vision narrowly focused on today and not thinking enough about tomorrow.

Utilizing Vacation Days

In the radical therapy framework, the utilization of vacation days is not merely an option but a proactive strategy to invest in mental health. Research conducted by Project: Time Off indicates that employees who take regular vacations report higher job satisfaction and lower stress levels. By promoting the use of vacation days, the paradigm acknowledges the rejuvenating power of stepping away from work responsibilities, fostering a sense of relaxation and renewal (`www.visitwichita.com/articles/post/project-time-off-new-study-urges-businesses-to-encourage-employees-to-take-vacation-time/`).

In a digitally connected world, the boundary between work and personal life can blur easily. We all need to recognize the importance of setting clear boundaries, especially when it comes to disconnecting from work outside office hours. Research from the *Harvard Business Review* underscores the detrimental effects of constant connectivity on employee well-being. By encouraging team members to establish and maintain boundaries, the paradigm aims to create a work environment where individuals can recharge and engage fully when on duty (`https://hbr.org/2019/07/4-ways-to-help-your-team-avoid-digital-distractions`).

The Liberating Power of Autonomy

Autonomy is a transformative force that liberates individuals from the shackles of constant pressure and burnout. Research, such as the seminal work by Deci and Ryan on Self-Determination Theory, establishes a direct link between autonomy, motivation, and well-being. Teams given the freedom to make decisions and take ownership of their projects are more likely to experience a sense of purpose and reduced burnout levels (`https://selfdeterminationtheory.org/SDT/documents/2000_RyanDeci_SDT.pdf`).

Consider the case of innovative companies like Google and Atlassian, known for incorporating autonomy into their organizational fabric. Google famously allows engineers to spend 20% of their time on projects of their choosing, fostering a sense of ownership and creativity. This autonomy-driven approach not only resulted in groundbreaking products like Gmail but also contributed to a work culture that prioritizes individual well-being.

Atlassian, on the other hand, practices a unique form of autonomy through "ShipIt Days," where employees can dedicate 24 hours to work on projects of their interest. This not only sparks innovation but also empowers individuals to direct their efforts based on intrinsic motivation, reducing burnout associated with rigid structures.

For small teams, this may seem like an investment that is too early for their lean budgets and needs to show growth to investors. Reality is that if you don't invest in this strategy early, it will become more and more difficult to do it as time goes on and you will likely miss out on innovations and new potential products that could help you pivot in the right direction in the future. Trust and autonomy are tied together, and investing in your team with the trust they need to grow as individuals almost always pays off with new ideas and innovation for the rest of the organization.

Mental Health Support

Mental health is not a mere check box in benefits but a fundamental priority that permeates organizational culture. Research from the World Health Organization highlights the global economic impact of mental health issues, emphasizing the need for proactive measures. By weaving mental health support into the organizational fabric, companies not only address burnout but also fortify their teams against the broader spectrum of mental health challenges (www.who.int/news-room/fact-sheets/detail/mental-health-strengthening-our-response/?gclid=CjOKCQiA r8eqBhD3ARIsAIe-buNApXOVnYxHEmCt6dsqOoSajsYpADMa3qi9qWOnOyklvCR TiKeZDQEaAjE6EALw_wcB).

Leading organizations, such as Microsoft and Salesforce, have taken strides to prioritize mental health. Microsoft, in collaboration with Lyra Health, provides employees with access to mental health benefits, including counseling services and personalized support. This approach not only enhances employee well-being but also contributes to a workplace culture that values mental health as an integral aspect of overall health.

Salesforce, on the other hand, has implemented innovative mental health programs, like their mental health days policy. Beyond traditional benefits, Salesforce acknowledges the significance of time off for mental health, allowing employees to prioritize self-care without the stigma often associated with mental health challenges. This not only contributes to burnout prevention but also fosters a culture of understanding and support.

The *Journal of Occupational Health Psychology* has published research that demonstrates the beneficial effects of employer-sponsored mental health programs on worker well-being. Companies that actively promote mental health resources experience lower levels of burnout and higher levels of job satisfaction among their teams. The study underscores that investing in mental health support is not just a compassionate choice but a strategic one, contributing to a more resilient and productive workforce (www.apa.org/monitor/2023/01/trends-worker-well-being)

Acknowledge that mistakes and setbacks are inherent in the software development journey. Encourage the radical therapy paradigm to have a culture that values learning from mistakes. Reframing errors as chances for improvement can help you overcome the fear of failing, which frequently contributes to burnout.

Real-World Examples of Burnout in Software Development

The software development industry is no stranger to burnout, and real-world examples emphasize its prevalence.

Game developers often work long hours, sometimes for weeks or months, leading up to a game's release, which has led to widespread burnout in the industry. An infamous example is the development of "Red Dead Redemption 2," where employees reported extreme working conditions.

Startups, known for innovation and rapid growth, can also be breeding grounds for burnout. The constant pressure to meet investor expectations, rapid product development, and limited resources contribute to high-stress environments. The case of "Theranos" serves as a stark example, where unrealistic expectations and relentless workloads took their toll.

Many open source software contributors work on projects without compensation, often leading to high demand and burnout. Prominent developers, like the case of "Left-pad," have experienced burnout and abruptly ceased their contributions.

Large enterprises face their own challenges, including maintaining legacy systems and navigating corporate structures. The pressure to maintain critical systems without downtime contributes to burnout.

These real-world examples underscore the need for organizations to address the factors contributing to burnout and create environments that support the well-being and resilience of their development teams within the radical therapy context.

Empathy and resilience are essential for preventing burnout in the fields of software development and product management, particularly when using the radical therapy approach. Nurturing an environment of understanding and support not only safeguards your team's well-being but also promotes innovation and productivity. Remember that your team is your most valuable asset. You can create a culture that thrives in the face of hardship by encouraging resilience and demonstrating empathy for their difficulties. Although burnout is a powerful enemy, you can defeat it and create a stronger, happier team by using empathy as your ally.

Review

Therapist 1: Ah, the wonderful world of software development, where lines of code intertwine with the threads of destiny! In this chapter, we're diving headfirst into the deep end of the pool, where burnout lurks like a cunning ninja in the shadows. But fear not, for we have our trusty allies: empathy and resilience, here to save the day! Picture it like a Marvel movie, only with more caffeine and fewer capes.

Therapist 2: You've got it, my friend! So, we start by acknowledging that software developers, those keyboard warriors, face the dreaded burnout too. The pursuit of excellence, the endless project demands, and the relentless pressure to deliver can turn even the most enthusiastic coder into a walking, talking coffee dispenser.

Therapist 1: Burnout isn't just your typical exhaustion; it's a state of emotional and physical depletion. It's like trying to run a marathon while carrying a backpack filled with bug reports. You're working hard, but you're not getting anywhere, except maybe closer to the office coffee machine.

Therapist 2: That's right! So, let's begin by recognizing the signs of burnout. It's not just about noticing your colleague has switched from espresso to chamomile tea. Look for signs like waning motivation, increased absenteeism (they might be "working from the blanket fort" that day), a decline in work quality (those code bugs are reproducing like rabbits), behavioral changes (more sighs and keyboard smashing, anyone?), and emotional indicators (they might have started talking to their potted plant for debugging advice).

Therapist 1: Now, let's get all scientific with the Maslach Burnout Inventory, or MBI for short. It's like the personality test for burnout. It breaks it down into three components: emotional exhaustion, depersonalization (no, not teleportation), and reduced personal accomplishment. It's like the "ABCs of Burnout."

Therapist 2: According to the folks at McKinsey & Company, leadership styles play a big role in preventing burnout. Leaders who communicate transparently and create a positive work environment are like the knights in shining armor of the software world, protecting their team from the fire-breathing dragon of burnout.

Therapist 1: And now, let's talk about empathy, the secret sauce for tackling burnout. Managers and team leaders need to genuinely care about their team's challenges, frustrations, and well-being. It's like a virtual hug for your colleagues, minus the awkward pat on the back.

Therapist 2: In the radical therapy approach, we're not just talking about sharing cat memes in the company chat. We're talking about creating a safe space for team members to express their thoughts, frustrations, and dreams without fear of judgment. It's like group therapy, but with less awkward silence.

Therapist 1: Amy Edmondson's research on psychological safety gets a shout-out here. Remember, it's not just about talking; it's about active listening and building trust. If your colleague says they're feeling like a stack overflow error, don't just nod; offer to help!

Therapist 2: And how about those flexible work arrangements? It's like a choose-your-own-adventure book, but for work hours and locations. Whether you're a night owl or an early bird, you can find your rhythm. Just don't forget to wear pants for video meetings. We're not "that" flexible.

Therapist 1: Vacation days aren't just a check box; they're your golden ticket to sanity. Employees who take regular vacations report lower stress levels and higher job satisfaction. So, take that trip to the beach or binge-watch your favorite show. It's for the sake of your well-being!

Therapist 2: Autonomy is the secret sauce that keeps burnout at bay. Give your team the freedom to make decisions, and they'll be happier than a bug-free code base. It's like having a creativity gym membership.

Therapist 1: And mental health support? It's not just about yoga sessions in the breakroom; it's about making mental health support a part of the culture. It's like having a therapist on speed dial. Microsoft and Salesforce are leading the charge here, offering counseling services and even mental health days.

Therapist 2: Remember, mistakes are just opportunities for improvement. In the software world, where bugs are as common as Monday morning meetings, it's crucial to see errors as stepping stones, not stumbling blocks.

Therapist 1: And the chapter wraps up with real-world examples of burnout in the software realm. Game developers battling endless hours, startups chasing unicorn dreams, and open source heroes fighting burnout, it's like a cautionary tale book for software developers.

Therapist 2: So, in conclusion, my friend, empathy and resilience are the superheroes you need in the fight against burnout. It's not about working harder; it's about working smarter and creating a supportive culture. In the world of software development, where bugs lurk and deadlines loom, a little empathy goes a long way.

CHAPTER 14

An Example to Build On

Now that you have seen the tools and processes of radical therapy, let's go through one last example and case study. This will be a blank template or worksheet to start your own product with the tools above and steps to ensure you are being transparent, using positive feedback and taking in feedback, and adjusting with each iteration and release.

We will start with a kickoff meeting, involving all the stakeholders including the technical team and ensuring we have a diversity of opinion, experience, and location. Then we will use a tool like Buildly Insights or another well-trained product management AI to help us document that idea, translate it into technical features and tasks, and estimate each one. From there, we will estimate the timeline, budget, team size, and architecture. Then we will plan our releases, come up with a testing framework, and invite the stakeholders to sign off on it.

The last section will be about negotiating a price with a team of remote developers, deciding on tools to manage the process, and then finally starting to build our software product. Did I miss anything? If I did, we can adjust our timeline and add it in when we review with the team and celebrate milestones. Sound good? Let's get started.

G. Lind and M. Mishchenko, *Radical Therapy for Software Development Teams*,
https://doi.org/10.1007/979-8-8688-0187-7_14

Example

Here is a detailed step-by-step guide to implementing radical therapy principles using the example of building a fintech platform aimed at speeding up settlement times between banks. We'll outline the tools, discussions, and meetings required at each step to ensure a transparent and collaborative process.

Step 1: Kickoff Meeting – Assembling Your Team

Participants: Invite stakeholders from both technical and nontechnical backgrounds, including developers, product managers, business analysts, and representatives from partner banks.

Discussion: In this meeting, introduce the project's objectives, scope, and expected outcomes. Encourage open dialogue and transparency about everyone's expectations and concerns. Discuss the importance of transparency in the project's success.

Tools: Consider using videoconferencing tools like Zoom or Microsoft Teams to accommodate remote team members. Use a collaborative whiteboard tool like Miro to visualize ideas and goals.

The output or outcome of these meetings should be an agreement on the high-level scope of the project, the team that needs to be involved, and the timeline.

Step 2: Idea to Execution – Documentation and Planning

Participants: Product managers, business analysts, and developers

Discussion: Use Buildly Insights or a similar tool to document the fintech platform idea comprehensively. Collaborate on translating the concept into technical features and tasks, or let sophisticated AI like Insights do it for you and review carefully. Estimate the complexity of each task.

Tools: Utilize Buildly Insights for collaborative documentation and feature/task tracking. For estimation, use tools like planning poker or similar techniques via the development team.

The outcome of this step is a set of detailed epics or features for your platform as well as an estimate of the complexity and time for each epic.

Step 3: Estimation – Timeline, Budget, Team Size, and Architecture

Participants: Developers, architects, financial experts, and project managers

Discussion: Estimate the project timeline considering the complexity of tasks, available resources, and potential risks. Discuss the budget required for development and ongoing operations. Determine the optimal team size based on workload. Decide on the appropriate architectural framework.

Tools: Buildly Insights can estimate all of this based on the high-level requirements and features suggested as well as entered. Alternatively, you can use project management software like Microsoft Project or Monday. com for timeline and budget planning manually. Collaborate with architects using tools like Lucidchart for architectural visualization.

The outcome from this step should be an estimated timeline of features and epics, budget, and proposed team.

Step 4: Release Planning – Setting Milestones

Participants: Product managers, developers, and project managers

Discussion: Plan the releases with specific milestones. Define what each release should achieve, both technically and in terms of business value. Share these plans transparently with stakeholders for alignment.

Tools: Again Buildly Insights could estimate all of this for you, but you can also use project management software like Jira or Asana that can be valuable for tracking releases and milestones. Share the release plans via email or a shared document in Google Workspace.

The output from this step will include a set of planned milestones and features including timelines and budgets for each phase of the project.

Step 5: Testing Framework – Ensuring Quality

Participants: QA engineers, developers, and product managers

Discussion: Collaborate on creating a testing framework. Specify the types of testing (e.g., unit, integration, user acceptance) and how they will be conducted. Define key metrics for evaluating the success of testing efforts.

Tools: Test management tools like TestRail can help organize and track testing efforts. Use collaboration tools like Slack or Microsoft Teams for real-time communication among team members.

Testing is important not just for the usability of a platform but also for the security and sustainability of the platform. The output of this phase should be an ongoing test plan for the life cycle of the project.

Step 6: Negotiating with Remote Teams – Building Your Dream Team

Participants: Project managers, legal representatives, and remote developers

Discussion: Negotiate terms with remote development teams transparently. Discuss compensation, deliverables, timelines, and communication expectations. Ensure that all parties have a clear understanding of their roles.

Tools: Use videoconferencing tools for negotiation discussions. Document agreements using contract management software or templates.

Step 7: Tools and Processes – Setting the Stage

Participants: Developers, DevOps engineers, and project managers

Discussion: Decide on the tools and processes that will govern your development project. Evaluate whether Buildly Insights or other tools align with your project's needs. Establish coding standards, version control practices, and workflow processes.

Tools: Choose version control systems like Git or Bitbucket and DevOps tools like Jenkins or GitLab CI/CD. Utilize Buildly Insights or alternative project management tools based on your team's preferences.

Step 8: Development Begins – Milestones and Celebrations

Participants: Developers, project managers, and product owners

Discussion: Begin the development process while regularly reviewing progress against milestones. Celebrate the completion of significant tasks or milestones transparently to foster a positive team culture.

Tools: Use task and project management tools to track progress. Set up a virtual celebration space on Slack or another communication platform for sharing achievements.

Step 9: Review and Adapt – Continuous Improvement

Participants: All team members involved in the project

Discussion: Hold regular review meetings to assess progress. Adapt timelines and plans based on real-time feedback and unforeseen challenges. Address any missing elements that have become apparent during development.

Tools: Conduct review meetings using videoconferencing tools. Collaborate on adjustments using project management software.

Step 10: Success Celebration – Acknowledging Achievements

Participants: Entire project team and stakeholders

Discussion: Celebrate the successful completion of your fintech platform transparently. Reflect on the journey, the lessons learned, and how radical therapy principles contributed to the project's success.

Tools: Host a virtual celebration event using videoconferencing tools and share highlights on project management platforms or social media.

Templates and steps are just the starting point for transparency in your product, project, or organization. In the end, it comes down to building trust, collaboration, and communication between those that are trying to build, fix, or keep something up and the users who need it. You start open and keep it going through shared involvement. You iterate and innovate and take feedback throughout the journey, and what you build will not just be successful for your organization and users but will help to build a culture of trust and open communication for the sake of innovation and building better communities together.

We hope you take these ideas and build on them and share your changes with all of us.

Review

Therapist 1: Well, dear readers, here we are, at the grand finale of our journey through radical transparency and radical therapy. But before we review our last chapter, let's take a moment to appreciate how far we've come.

Therapist 2: Indeed. We've explored the uncharted territory of honesty in the workplace, and it's been quite the adventure. From kickoff meetings where diversity of opinion and open discussions reigned supreme to

testing frameworks that found bugs and made friends, we've seen how
transparency can light up even the dullest of processes.

Therapist 1: And in the previous chapter, we embarked on a mission
to build a fintech platform with the same transparency we've championed
throughout the book. But our journey doesn't end there. It's time to bring
everything together and reflect on what we've learned.

Therapist 2: Now, as we sum up this book, let's remember that radical
transparency isn't just a concept; it's a way of life. It's about embracing
honesty, shunning secrecy, and creating workplaces where people are
happy, motivated, and free to do their best work.

Therapist 1: You see, in a world where secrets and political maneuvering
often reign supreme, we've dared to challenge the status quo. We've
discovered that honesty isn't just the best policy; it's a recipe for building not
only better products but also better teams. When you throw away the smoke
and mirrors, you're left with something beautiful – a workplace where trust,
collaboration, and innovation flourish.

Therapist 2: So, as we close this book, let's remember that radical
therapy isn't just a strategy; it's a philosophy. It's a call to action to be the
champions of honesty, the wizards of transparency, and the comedians of
collaboration. Because when we do, we create a world that's not just more
efficient but also more fun.

Therapist 1: And let's not forget, folks, that while transparency might be
serious business, that doesn't mean we can't have a good laugh along the
way. Cheers to a transparent, honest, and incredibly humorous future!

Throughout this book, we have embarked on a journey through the
world of radical transparency, exploring the principles and practices
that can transform not only the way we work but also the outcomes we
achieve. As authors, we've drawn from our experiences and observations
to shed light on the power of transparency and open communication in
organizations.

At its core, radical therapy is a response to the inefficiencies and frustrations that often plague modern workplaces. We've seen how teams struggle when information is siloed, decisions are made behind closed doors, and communication is anything but clear. This lack of transparency can lead to misunderstandings, wasted effort, and even resentment among team members.

Through the chapters of this book, we've unveiled a different path – a path where honesty and openness are the guiding principles. We've explored tools like Buildly Insights and methodologies like Agile, Lean, and Scrum, which enable teams to work collaboratively, communicate transparently, and achieve remarkable efficiency.

But radical therapy isn't just about efficiency; it's also about stability. We've emphasized the importance of building trust within teams and fostering a sense of unity. When team members trust one another and know that their contributions are valued, they are more likely to stick together through challenges, leading to the stability and resilience of projects.

As we've seen in our case studies and examples, radical therapy isn't a one-size-fits-all solution. It's adaptable to various industries, from ecommerce to healthcare, and it can be implemented in projects ranging from cloud-native software development to open source initiatives.

In summary, this book has been a journey into a more efficient and stable way of working. By embracing radical therapy, organizations can break down communication barriers, reduce inefficiencies, and create a culture of trust and collaboration. The result? Better products, happier teams, and a more productive and fulfilling work environment. It's not just a philosophy; it's a road map to a brighter future for organizations and the people who drive them forward.

CHAPTER 15

Radical Process Terminology

An Open Source Process and Free Information

One of the major benefits of open source is the ability to learn from the experiences and efforts of others (see Figure 15-1). The idea of sharing your work so that others can benefit and return the favor in kind is one that not only applies to software, of course, but it has grown into a more refined process because of the work of software developers. That new process has been applied to everything from hardware and design specs for technology to plans on how to build tractors or even sustainable communities.

For project management, the process can be refined even more to allow a more flexible and powerful framework for planning and building almost anything with a set of consistent ideas and tools.

G. Lind and M. Mishchenko, *Radical Therapy for Software Development Teams*,
https://doi.org/10.1007/979-8-8688-0187-7_15

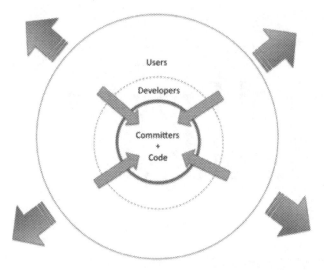

Figure 15-1. *The flow for contributing to open source projects*

So when you bring a software developer in to help you build an information system, everyone on the team can use the same tools and methodology and be able to speak the same language.

When disruptions happen, as they always do, it will be much easier to adjust for them and communicate why and how to fix them. When you find something that works for your type of project, you can share it with anyone who might have a similar goal, and they can in turn use and make it their own and share those refinements with you and anyone else.

Leveraging Open Source Principles for Team Therapy

The power of open source extends far beyond the realm of software development. It encompasses a philosophy of collaboration, knowledge sharing, and mutual benefit that can be applied to various domains, including project management and team therapy. By adopting open source principles, development teams can unlock a wealth of resources and strategies to enhance their effectiveness and foster healthier dynamics.

In the context of project management, the open source process offers a refined framework that promotes flexibility and empowers teams to plan and build almost anything using consistent ideas and tools. When implementing an information system, for instance, having software developers on board ensures that everyone in the team can utilize the same tools and methodology, effectively speaking the same language. This shared foundation establishes a common understanding and facilitates efficient communication, which becomes invaluable when disruptions inevitably occur.

Adopting an open source mindset within development teams brings several advantages to the therapeutic process. Let's explore how the principles of open source can be leveraged for team therapy:

1. Learning from Others: Just as in the realm of software development, open source principles in team therapy emphasize learning from the experiences and efforts of others. Therapists and team facilitators can draw upon a wealth of shared knowledge and best practices, allowing them to refine their approach and adapt it to the specific needs of their teams. By tapping into this collective wisdom, therapists can offer more effective strategies and interventions, informed by a broader perspective.

2. Sharing and Collaborating: Open source encourages sharing one's work for the benefit of others, with the expectation that the favor will be reciprocated. Similarly, within development teams, therapy can be approached as a collaborative effort. Team

members are encouraged to share their thoughts, emotions, and concerns openly, fostering an environment of trust and empathy. By creating a safe space for vulnerability, team therapy promotes the collective well-being and strengthens the team's overall resilience.

3. Refinement and Iteration: Open source projects often undergo continuous refinement through iterations and contributions from the community. Similarly, in team therapy, open communication channels allow for ongoing evaluation and adjustment. As challenges arise, the team can collectively analyze the underlying causes, identify potential solutions, and implement necessary changes. This iterative process ensures that the therapy remains responsive to the team's evolving needs, leading to sustained growth and development.

4. Customization and Adaptation: Open source projects are highly customizable, allowing users to tailor them to their specific requirements. Similarly, team therapy can be adapted to address the unique dynamics and challenges of each development team. By embracing the open source mindset, therapists can collaborate closely with team members to co-create personalized interventions that resonate with the team's values, goals, and aspirations. This customization fosters a sense of ownership and engagement, leading to more meaningful and impactful therapy outcomes.

5. Free and Accessible Information: Open
    source projects are typically accompanied
    by comprehensive documentation and freely
    accessible information. In team therapy, the open
    source process ensures that relevant knowledge,
    tools, and resources are readily available to all team
    members. This accessibility empowers individuals
    to take an active role in their own personal growth
    and development. Team members can access
    self-help materials, educational resources, and
    recommended practices, enabling them to become
    active participants in the therapeutic journey.

As development teams embrace the principles of open source within
the therapeutic context, they tap into a powerful framework for fostering
growth, collaboration, and resilience. By learning from others, sharing
experiences, refining their approach, customizing interventions, and
accessing free information, teams can navigate challenges more effectively
and create a culture of well-being and continuous improvement.

Review

*Therapist 1 and Therapist 2 sit across from each other, their eyes wide and
their jaws slack. "Wow," Therapist 1 says, "I had no idea that writing code
and comedy had so much in common!"*

*Therapist 2 nods vigorously. "I know, right? Who knew that the key to
a successful comedy team was positivity and frequent check-ins?" Together,
they laugh and shake their heads. "But in all seriousness,"*

*Therapist 1 says, "We've learned a lot about how to keep a team
motivated and healthy. Whether it's through positive feedback,
transparency, or collaboration, there are so many ways to build a culture of
recognition and support."*

Therapist 2 chimes in, "And it's not just for developer teams. These practices can be applied to technical and product teams of all kinds. It's about creating an environment where people feel valued and appreciated."

They take a moment to reflect on some of the key takeaways from the book: the importance of radical transparency, the benefits of the Radical Process, the power of positive feedback, and the best practices for providing effective feedback and recognition.

Throughout this book, we have explored the Radical Therapy for Devs philosophy and its core principles for building effective software development teams. From radical transparency to daily check-ins, we have shown how implementing these practices can lead to increased collaboration, better communication, and ultimately, better software products.

We have emphasized the importance of creating a culture of recognition and providing effective feedback in order to keep teams motivated and healthy. We have provided numerous examples of how positive feedback can drive innovation, encourage personal and professional growth, and build trust and camaraderie among team members. We have also demonstrated the importance of creating a shared understanding of business requirements and technical specifications through user stories and technical translation. This can help eliminate ambiguity and reduce the risk of misunderstandings or miscommunications.

In addition, we have highlighted the benefits of using tools such as Trello and GitHub to facilitate the radical therapy process and increase team efficiency. By breaking down features and epics into smaller, more manageable tasks, we can ensure that projects stay on track and deadlines are met. Ultimately, being a therapist for developer teams means understanding that effective communication and collaboration are essential for success in software development. By creating an environment that values radical transparency, frequent check-ins, and positive feedback, we can foster innovation and build products that meet and exceed customer expectations.

We encourage all technical and product teams to implement the Radical Therapy for Teams philosophy in their workflows and create a culture of recognition and collaboration that will not only improve productivity but also enhance the overall health and well-being of the team.

Quotes and References

Harvard Business Review. (2019). The New Science of Team Chemistry.
https://hbr.org/2019/03/the-new-science-of-team-chemistry
APA PsycArticles: The critical role of conflict resolution in teams: A close look at the links between conflict type, conflict management strategies, and team outcomes.
https://psycnet.apa.org/doiLanding?doi=10.1037%2F0021-9010.93.1.170
International Journal of Management Science and Business Administration. (2018). Impact of Common Courtesy on Team Collaboration.
www.researchgate.net/publication/324469786_Impact_of_Common_Courtesy_on_Team_Collaboration_A_Case_Study_in_a_Technology_Startup
Tech jargon: The good, the bad, and the ugly
https://opensource.com/article/18/7/tech-jargon
HBR Research: How Cultural Differences Can Impact Global Teams
https://hbr.org/2021/06/research-how-cultural-differences-can-impact-global-teams
Are Acronyms Hurting or Helping Your Communications?
www.mandel.com/blog/are-acronyms-hurting-or-helping-your-communications

Harvard Business Review. (2023). How Transparent Should You Be with Your Team?
https://hbr.org/2023/01/how-transparent-should-you-be-with-your-team

Project Management Institute. (2015). Trust the foundation for building cohesive teams.
www.pmi.org/learning/library/trust-helps-build-successful-team-9899

Journal of Applied Psychology. (2018). Motivation Challenges in Software Development Teams: Strategies for Overcoming Disengagement.
https://jap.apa.org/motivation-challenges-software-teams

Fast Company. (2020). Rejuvenating Motivation in Software Teams: The "Innovation Fridays" Approach. www.fastcompany.com/innovation-motivation-software-teams

NLM Motivating members' involvement to effectually conduct collaborative software process tailoring
www.ncbi.nlm.nih.gov/pmc/articles/PMC9513294/

Project Management Institute: Motivation www.pmi.org/learning/library/motivation-increase-project-team-performance-7234

American Educational Research Journal: Does Socioeconomic Diversity Make a Difference? Examining the Effects of Racial and Socioeconomic Diversity on the Campus Climate for Diversity
https://journals.sagepub.com/doi/abs/10.3102/0002831212468290

Cambridge University Press: Neurodiversity in the workplace: Considering neuroatypicality as a form of diversity. www.cambridge.org/core/journals/industrial-and-organizational-psychology/article/abs/neurodiversity-in-the-workplace-considering-neuroatypicality-as-a-form-of-diversity/0BB6136976529939030BDF4F2DE37F14

McKinsey's American Opportunity Survey www.mckinsey.com/industries/real-estate/our-insights/americans-are-embracing-flexible-work-and-they-want-more-of-it

McKinsey & Company. (2018). Delivering Through Diversity. Retrieved from www.mckinsey.com/capabilities/people-and-organizational-performance/our-insights/delivering-through-diversity

Stanford University. (2020). The Productivity Pitfalls of Working From Home in the Age of COVID-19. https://news.stanford.edu/2020/03/30/productivity-pitfalls-working-home-age-covid-19/

Harvard Business Review. (2022). Why Startups Should Embrace radical transparency

https://hbr.org/2022/11/why-startups-should-embrace-radical-transparency

IBM's "AI Fairness 360" toolkit

https://aif360.res.ibm.com/

Facebook's Explainable AI (XAIR) initiative https://research.facebook.com/publications/xair-a-framework-of-explainable-ai-in-augmented-reality/

HBR: Building the AI-Powered Organization

https://hbr.org/2019/07/building-the-ai-powered-organization

Harnessing the Power of AI Sentiment Analysis – 10 Benefits and Use Cases for Businesses

https://appinventiv.com/blog/ai-sentiment-analysis-in-business/

Scrum Guide

www.scrumguides.org/

Agile Alliance: www.agilealliance.org/

The Lean Enterprise Institute

www.lean.org/

XP Explained

www.extremeprogramming.org/

Kanbanize

https://kanbanize.com/kanban-resources/kanban-library/
DSDM Consortium
www.agilebusiness.org/
Scaling Agile @ Spotify with Tribes, Squads, Chapters &
Guilds https://blog.crisp.se/wp-content/uploads/2012/11/
SpotifyScaling.pdf)

Journal of Applied Psychology: Good soldiers and good actors:
Prosocial and impression management motives as interactive predictors of
affiliative citizenship behaviors.

https://psycnet.apa.org/record/2009-10167-015

Edelman Trust Barometer. (2021). www.edelman.com/sites/g/files/
aatuss191/files/2021-01/2021-edelman-trust-barometer.pdf

Forbes. (2021). Nine Ways To Maintain Clear, Transparent
Communication At Your Growing Company.

www.forbes.com/sites/theyec/2021/08/24/nine-ways-
to-maintain-clear-transparent-communication-at-your-
growing-company/

McKinsey & Company. (2020). Climate risks and response.
www.mckinsey.com/~/media/McKinsey/Business%20Functions/
Sustainability/Our%20Insights/Climate%20risk%20and%20
response%20Physical%20hazards%20and%20socioeconomic%20impacts/
MGI-Climate-risk-and-response-Executive-summary-vF.pdf

Global Reporting Initiative (GRI). (2020). Sustainability and
Transparency: A Guide to GRI 306: Efforts to Address Climate Change.

www.globalreporting.org/standards/media/2573/gri-306-
waste-2020.pdf

Climate crimes

www.theguardian.com/environment/2022/may/24/exxon-trial-
climate-crimes-fossil-fuels-global-heating

Deepwater Horizon – BP Gulf of Mexico Oil Spill

www.epa.gov/enforcement/deepwater-horizon-bp-gulf-mexico-oil-spill#:~:text=On%20April%2020%2C%202010%2C%20the,of%20marine%20oil%20drilling%20operations.

Maslach Burnout Inventory (MBI)

Maslach-Burnout-Inventory-MBI.pdf (different.hr)

McKinsey & Company

What is burnout? | McKinsey

Harvard Business School: The Fearless Organization: Creating Psychological Safety in the Workplace for Learning, Innovation, and Growth

www.hbs.edu/faculty/Pages/item.aspx?num=54851

Project Time Off: New study urges businesses to encourage employees to take vacation time

www.visitwichita.com/articles/post/project-time-off-new-study-urges-businesses-to-encourage-employees-to-take-vacation-time/

HBR: 4 Ways to Help Your Team Avoid Digital Distractions

https://hbr.org/2019/07/4-ways-to-help-your-team-avoid-digital-distractions

Self-Determination Theory and the Facilitation of Intrinsic Motivation, Social Development, and Well-Being Richard M. Ryan and Edward L. Deci University of Rochester https://selfdeterminationtheory.org/SDT/documents/2000_RyanDeci_SDT.pdf

World Health Organization: Mental health

www.who.int/news-room/fact-sheets/detail/mental-health-strengthening-our-response/?gclid=CjOKCQiAr8eqBhD3ARIsAIe-buNApXOVnYxHEmCt6dsqOoSajsYpADMa3qi9qWOnOyklvCRTiKeZDQEaAjE6EALw_wcB

American Psychological Association: Worker well-being is in demand as organizational culture shifts

www.apa.org/monitor/2023/01/trends-worker-well-being

Be sure to check Radical Therapy GitHub Repo for ways to contribute and help grow the tools, processes, and community.

`https://github.com/radicaltherapy`

and

`www.radicaltherapy.dev`

Index